Academic Word Lists

Academic Word Lists

What Every ESL Teacher Needs to Know

By

Keith S. Folse

University of Michigan Press
Ann Arbor

First paperback published 2023
Copyright © Keith S. Folse, 2020
All rights reserved
Published in the United States of America by the
University of Michigan Press

First published March 2020

Paperback ISBN: 978-0-472-03952-4
Ebook ISBN: 978-0-472-12567-8

Printed and bound by CPI Group (UK) Ltd, Croydon, CR0 4YY

CONTENTS

A Brief Introduction

Vocabulary is an essential part of learning any new language. Learners certainly recognize the importance of vocabulary. In a study (Folse, 2010) of 50 hours of ESL classes taught by 10 different instructors, the number one question students asked during class was "What does (that word) mean?" To help students learn the vocabulary they need, many teachers, curriculum designers, and textbook writers use word lists. Lists are convenient, and many students really like word lists (Folse, 2004). In this work on academic word lists, we will look at what factors help produce vocabulary lists that are both accurate and practical.

In contrast to what students say about lists, some educators are fundamentally opposed to using word lists. As an experienced language teacher, but more importantly as an experienced learner of six foreign languages, I believe this idea is unfortunate and largely unfounded. As a result, in *Vocabulary Myths* (Folse, 2004), I dedicate a whole chapter to debunking the pervasive myth that word lists are bad.

Some teachers may say that learning from a list can be boring, and this is certainly true, but this appraisal is not limited to word lists. Sometimes the problem is not the list per se, but rather what the teacher and students do with the word list. Later in this book, I will discuss several useful, practical ideas for using an academic word list for both in-class and after-class study, but let's focus our discussion of word lists now by dismissing the simple notion that word lists are inherently bad learning opportunities. This is just not so.

For some teachers, word lists are bad because the words are out of context, but this notion assumes that having the word in a lengthy context is magically better. In fact, there is ample evidence to the contrary. When learning a new word, less information, such as synonyms (*dozen* = twelve) or simple phrases (*a dozen eggs* to remember the word *dozen*), is better than longer or more elaborated context.

In a study of Hebrew speakers learning English, Laufer and Shmueli (1997) compared four ways of presenting new words: (1) words in isolation in a word list, (2) words in one meaningful sentence, (3) words in text context, and (4) words in elaborated text context. They found that words presented in lists and in sentences were remembered better than words presented in text and elaborated text. In this study, less information was better.

Another potential problem with word lists is that many learners simply memorize the words without any real thought about how those words might be used. In other words, learners do not interact with the new word, or imagine using it in a sentence or reading it in a book. If learners' only goal is to memorize a word, then teachers should not be surprised when students cannot actually *use* the words in speaking, listening, reading, or writing. Again, this is not a limitation of the list but rather of our learners' approaches and goals of using a word list. It also means that teachers must train students to understand how to study more effectively with a word list. (See Chapter 8, "Ten Classroom Suggestions" for specific ideas.) The truth is that a good word list, one that is based on actual English usage and learner needs, can be a very important tool in improving language proficiency.

The most widely used list in many ESL programs, especially English for Academic Purposes (EAP) programs, is the Academic Word List (AWL) (Coxhead, 2000), which was developed for students entering a college or university. Of course other word lists existed before the AWL was published in 2000, but the AWL was unique in that its words were identified using a very large collection, or corpus, of academic texts instead of being based mostly on human intuition. Over time, the AWL has become the standard for word lists for English learners, so much so that all new lists are based on the core methodology used by Coxhead in creating the AWL.

In many K–12 programs, however, vocabulary selection is not based on a corpus of student texts. Instead, it appears that intuition is used to determine whether a word should or should not be given instruction time, based on a three-tiered vocabulary classification system in which words can be classified as Tier 1, Tier 2, or Tier 3 (Beck et al., 2013). Rather than giving a specific list like the AWL, the authors provide a general description of each tier and allow teachers to determine the classification of a given word. One immediate problem with this situation is that different teachers will classify different words with different tiers, so ultimately there is no way to know if any teacher is in fact focusing on words that students really need.

The descriptors given to teachers to help label a word as 1, 2, or 3 are quite vague. Common words that most student already knew when they enter school and therefore require very little instructional time are called Tier 1. Words that are important across different academic content areas are called Tier 2. Finally, words that are specific to a certain content area are Tier 3. Because this system is not based on actual measurable categories, it does not at all offer the same accuracy as the AWL or other corpus-based academic lists that are derived from actual data, not just general descriptions. In fact, in reading about Tier 2 words, many school websites say that academic words are Tier 2 words because Tier 2 words are academic words, which says nothing. In effect, it is a circle. Even though Common Core Standards documents focus on the importance of teaching Tier 2 words, there is no clear list of words.

When K–12 programs are given a specific list, it is still not based on a corpus of student materials such as their textbooks or writing assignments. In *Building Academic Vocabulary*, Marzano and Pickering (2005) provide a list of 7,923 terms for 11 subject areas: mathematics, science, English language arts, history, geography, civics, economics, health, physical education, the arts, and technology. These 7,923 terms are further divided into four levels: Grades K–2, 3–5, 6–8, 9–12. Despite the impressive size, subject areas, and grade levels, there is no evidence these words came from material that students have to read, such as a corpus of student textbooks, let alone any other kind of corpus of daily academic language. Instead, Marzano and Pickering (2005) tell us these words were "extracted from national standards documents" (p. 5). Worse, we are then told that "some might not be found in your state-level standards" (p. 5), and "not all terms (even if found in your state standards documents) are of equal importance" (p. 5). These shortcomings are exactly why we need *corpus-based* lists, not just lists.

Teachers know their students need academic language, especially vocabulary. When I conduct talks and workshops on teaching vocabulary, teachers invariably ask me three questions: 1) Which words should I teach to my (high school / university / writing / conversation) students? 2) Do you have a list of these words? 3) How should I teach (or practice) these words in my classes? The purpose of this book is to answer these three important questions and thereby help teachers know more about useful academic vocabulary lists (such as the AWL) and how these lists can be used effectively to improve learning.

1. Why Are Word Lists Useful in Language Learning?

The Importance of Vocabulary

Communicating in any language requires good vocabulary knowledge. If learners mispronounce a certain sound in English, a native speaker might notice their accent. If learners make a grammar error in a sentence, a native speaker may realize the non-native language but can usually follow what they are trying to say. However, if learners mess up vocabulary—for example, they cannot remember a certain word or they use the wrong word—communication may in fact stop. The bottom line is that in speaking or writing, vocabulary matters. Vocabulary matters tremendously. Not knowing a word for something can instantly derail anyone's message.

Native English speakers take years to acquire the hundreds of thousands of words, idioms, and phrases they know (Nagy & Herman, 1987), yet our English learners know only a fraction of this vocabulary in their new language (Folse, 2004). What can they do to catch up? What can we teachers do to help them catch up? Broadly speaking, there are two very different big-picture approaches to this situation: learning vocabulary from natural input, or learning vocabulary from explicit instruction.

Acquiring Vocabulary Through the Natural Approach

One way to increase vocabulary knowledge is based on exposure to natural language, that is, to have students read or listen to English so they will be exposed to a lot of good input. Through this input, it was thought that students would acquire English naturally, just as we all did in our native languages (Krashen & Terrell, 1983). We use the word *acquire* because learners are not intentionally trying to learn anything.

One support for this **Natural Approach** (Terrell, 1977; Krashen & Terrell, 1983) is that the vast majority of the words you and I use in our native languages every day (English, in my case) are not words anyone ever taught us. Instead, they are most likely words we simply acquired through our daily interactions in our native language, with rich input all around us over multiple years. This natural approach has worked because we met the two required conditions: lots of input and lots of time.

The Natural Approach dominated thought in language education in the 1980s and into the early '90s. Teachers were told to help students acquire English speaking and listening through natural input, much as we all had done in our native languages—that is, without formal instruction of any kind from our parents, friends, or teachers. As a result, any lesson that included a focus on grammar, spelling, or word lists was considered ineffective and actually taboo since it was not natural. As a result, books could not include word lists and teachers did not explicitly teach vocabulary. While our current attention to vocabulary in language learning may seem normal today, there was an unfortunate period in language education when teachers were told that using lists—or explicit teaching of any kind for that matter—was unproductive and possibly harmful.

The Natural Approach was an attempt to replicate in the second language classroom what native speakers do in acquiring their first language. However, first language (L1) acquisition and second language (L2) learning are not the same (Cook, 2010; Meisel, 2011), and what is natural in one is not necessarily good (or bad) in the other. In fact, L2 acquisition is extremely complex, involving an array of factors that at different times work individually, cooperatively, and sometimes contradictorily (Lightbown, 1985). Simply put, acquiring L1 is not the same as learning L2.

Learning Vocabulary Through Explicit Instruction

A second option to help students learn vocabulary is to provide **explicit instruction**. This instruction can be done in many different ways. One way is for the teacher to write 10 adjectives on the board and explain them with examples relevant to the students. Another way is for the teacher to also ask students to look up the 10 adjectives in a dictionary (electronic, web-based, or paper) and then sort the words into adjectives with positive, neutral, or negative connotations.

Any form of intentional learning is considered explicit instruction. If students are told to look up a translation for each of the 10 adjectives and then study the words, this is explicit instruction, albeit without an instructor. In ESL classes, the most usual form of explicit instruction is a teacher explaining vocabulary to the class.

Which Option Is Better for Rapid L2 Vocabulary Growth?

The requisite conditions for the Natural Approach to succeed—lots of input and lots of time—are unfortunately almost impossible for many English learners to meet. Learners are rarely, if ever, surrounded by multiple native speakers who can provide the level of extensive rich input and interaction that young native speakers have access to when acquiring their native languages naturally.

This situation is true for learners in both EFL and ESL settings. If they are in an EFL setting such as China or Brazil, they probably hear or see English very little on a daily basis. In an ESL setting such as the U.S. or Canada, students tend to be exposed to English in class for up to five hours per day (in an ideal setting), but then often end up speaking their native language as soon as they leave class. Even in an intensive English program (IEP) where learners have paid large sums of money to study English, their exposure to English outside of class can vary tremendously. Human nature dictates that few students are going to speak English with their friends or family when they share the same native language.

Furthermore, our learners do not have the luxury of time that the natural approach requires. English learners face a tremendous time crunch, a situation that Cobb (1999) sums up well: "students typically need to know words measured in thousands, not hundreds, but receive language instruction measured in months, not years" (p. 345). We are all living proof that the natural approach works for native speakers acquiring our native languages, but the natural approach takes years. In most cases, our learners do not have years. In some cases, for instance, they need to pass a high-stakes exam in English in the very near future.

To be clear, both the natural approach and explicit instruction result in students learning vocabulary, but if you do not have lots of input at the right level as well as lots of time, the natural approach is not really a viable option for most English learners. Fortunately, many research studies in ESL, EFL, and EAP settings have shown that our second option, explicit vocabulary instruction, is in fact effective in improving vocabulary learning (Ebadi et al., 2018; Eckerth & Tavakoli, 2012; Hill & Laufer, 2003; Sonbul & Schmitt, 2010; Zimmerman, 1997), so explicit vocabulary instruction should definitely be a component of all English programs. However, in order to explicitly focus on vocabulary, we need a list of important, relevant words for instruction.

A Corpus

Given that students have limited time to learn a lot of vocabulary, we need an effective, practical way to determine which words should be the focus of our explicit instruction. It is easy to say that learners need to focus on "important vocabulary," but how will we determine which vocabulary is important and which is not? Learners need to learn high-frequency words, phrases, and idioms, but they also need vocabulary for their specific language needs. For example, if students need to comprehend lectures in a university biology class, then they need to learn key vocabulary that is common in university biology lectures. In short, they need a well-constructed list that matches their English vocabulary needs.

At this point, you may be thinking, "Teachers and textbook writers have been creating useful word lists for years, so let's just use one of those lists." Yes, teachers and textbook writers have compiled word lists, but until recently, these lists were usually based on one person's intuition or hunch as to which vocabulary is important. In other words, word selection was subjective, which is why there was no standard list for such a long time.

Instead of relying on human intuition, however, more recent lists use modern computer programs to identify the most frequent vocabulary from extremely large collections of real language. To continue with our previous example involving biology lectures, we would obtain transcripts of multiple biology lectures by various instructors of the same course. We might collect enough transcripts to assemble 500,000 to 1,000,000 or more words. This "body" of real language we have collected based on our students' needs (in this case, biology lectures) is called a **corpus** (Latin for *body*), so what students and teachers really need is a **corpus-based list**.

What kind of corpus should we use? As with many teaching questions, the correct answer depends on learner needs. A corpus-based analysis is only as reliable as the corpus is representative of the targeted language as a whole (Biber, 1993).

Our examples so far have been about biology lectures, but a corpus can vary based on student needs. Why are they learning English? For EAP students needing help being able to comprehend university lectures, we could use lecture transcripts like those found in the Michigan Corpus of Academic Spoken English (MICASE) (https://quod.lib.umich.edu/m/micase/). We should use a corpus of lectures, not readings, because these students need to practice the vocabulary they are likely to hear in a university lecture setting, not necessarily the vocabulary from their textbook, as these two vocabularies likely differ (Dang et al., 2017). In contrast, if students are trying to improve their general conversation skills, we might create a corpus of transcripts of real, unplanned, natural conversations, such as those in the Santa Barbara Corpus of Spoken American English (https://www.linguistics.ucsb.edu/research/santa-barbara-corpus).

In all cases, we should use a corpus that mirrors our students' actual English needs in terms of subject matter or topic (general academic, high school biology, basic English) and skill (listening, speaking, reading, writing). If the corpus addresses these areas, then we increase the chance of creating a good word list.

2. How Serious Is Our Students' Lexical Gap?

Our Students' Lexical Gap

To function in any new language, learners need vocabulary—and lots of it. How much vocabulary do learners need? How much vocabulary do learners already know? In answering these two questions, this section focuses on the lexical gap our students face between the vocabulary they know and the vocabulary they need to know to succeed academically (Laufer, 1997; Peters & Webb, 2018). Understanding this gap can guide us in producing a better vocabulary list that better meets our students' goals.

How much vocabulary does an English speaker know? A large study of more than two million people published in *The Economist* (G., 2013) found that the average adult native speaker of English knows about 27,500 words, yet an adult non-native speaker knows only about 4,500 English words, so the lexical gap between the two groups is quite substantial. As the article points out, even an average four-year-old native speaker already knows 5,000 words and an average eight-year-old knows a staggering 10,000 English words.

To English teachers and students, these figures may seem daunting and even demoralizing, but we should remember that our learners are not trying to become native speakers but rather to function well in their academic courses. Thus, the real question is how many words people actually need to speak well, to read well, to write well, and to listen well—that is, to function in an academic setting. In fact, the most frequent words are so frequent that they provide a very large coverage of a text. According to Nation (2006), knowing the 2,000 most frequent words should allow learners to recognize 70–90 percent of the words in English and therefore might motivate them to study further. Clearly, focusing on the 2,000 most frequent words is a very good beginning to help students.

A Word Is Not Just a Word: Different Kinds of Words

When most teachers think of *vocabulary* or *vocabulary list*, we tend to focus on individual or single words. In essence, *vocabulary = word*, but what exactly is a word? Traditionally, a word is limited to just a single collection of letters with a white space on each side (Folse, 2004), but this is not a practical definition at all. Vocabulary instruction also includes **compound words** (*website, living room*), **idioms** (*small potatoes, out of the blue*) (Macis & Schmitt, 2016); **sentence frames** (_____ *means to* _____), **lexical chunks** (*to make a long story short*), **phrasal verbs** (*take up, call off, come down with*) (Garnier & Schmitt, 2015); **collocations** (*deep sleep* instead of *strong sleep*) (Hsu & Chiu, 2008), and other formulaic language (Nattinger & DeCarrico, 1992; Wray, 2002). In addition to an individual word, academic language also includes all of these different types of phrases, as can be seen in the very robust Oxford Phrasal Academic Lexicon, or OPAL (retrieved from https://www.oxfordlearnersdictionaries.com/us/wordlists/opal).

Let's consider the lexical burden students face with just one of these lexical items: *out of the blue*. Each of these four individual words—*out, of, the, blue*—is a very frequent word in English. All four are likely known by most beginning and certainly all intermediate English learners, yet very few of these same learners would know the idiom *out of the blue*. Understanding *out* or *blue*, for example, does not in any way help you automatically know this idiom (though it may help students to remember the meaning of the phrase when it is being taught; *out of the blue* means "happening suddenly," as when something suddenly falls *out of the blue* sky). Unfortunately, our students' lack of knowledge of many common prefabricated expressions in English certainly contributes to their lexical dilemma.

Academic Vocabulary

In addition to all these different types of words, English learners in an academic setting, whether it be high school or a university class, also need to master the language used in an academic setting, which is loosely referred to as **academic vocabulary**.

A quick perusal of various online education sites produces the general consensus that academic vocabulary is the vocabulary that is common in academic settings, but is not as common in informal language. While perhaps accurate, this definition is too vague to help anyone determine whether one vocabulary item is academic while another is not (Baumann & Graves, 2010). For example, which words in this paragraph that you are reading right now would be considered academic? Why? Two teachers planning to pre-teach vocabulary will disagree on which words to focus on. The answer will vary according to who is doing the counting and what guidelines are being used to discriminate between general and academic vocabulary.

Well-known language expert Jim Cummins (2000) defines **academic language** as "the sum of vocabulary, grammatical constructions, and language functions that students will encounter and be required to demonstrate mastery of during their school years" (p. 541). When I first heard the term *academic language*, I remember thinking of words like *hypotenuse, chromosome,* and *treaty*. Yes, these words do occur in academic courses, but each word is pretty much confined to one subject. Thus, these three words are considered discipline-specific words, but not general academic language. For example, *hypotenuse* is limited to geometry, *chromosome* could appear frequently in biology, and *treaty* might be found in a history course. Good word lists would exclude these words, however, because they are not frequent in a large corpus containing words from many university subjects combined. The words in a good academic vocabulary list are meant to be useful for a wide array of students who need vocabulary for general academic purposes—that is, for a variety of college or university courses that a student might take.

To be clear, our EAP students need solid knowledge of words and phrases that are especially frequent in academic contexts such as textbooks or class lectures:

> While acquiring these lexical items is essential to the academic achievement of both native and non-native students, they represent a particularly significant hurdle for [second language] users, who have to understand and produce academic language in a language that is not their own.
>
> (Granger, 2017, p. 9)

Corpus-based word lists are one way in which educators can help our academic learners be better prepared for academic success.

3. A Timeline of the AWL

Word Lists Prior to the Creation of the AWL

For most teachers, the proverbial million-dollar question about L2 vocabulary has always been "Which words do my students need to know?" To answer this question, researchers developed lists based on word frequency.

A very good early example of this is the General Service List (GSL) (West, 1953), which was one of the first corpus-based lists in L2 English teaching and which for decades has been a guiding tool in determining the level of difficulty of reading passages. The GSL is a corpus-based list of approximately 2,200 words that were selected for English language learners and teachers. It was thought that with these 2,200 words, a learner could do well in English, hence the words were of "general service" for English learners. In fact, these words are extremely important because approximately 80 percent of all texts consist of these GSL words (Brezina & Gablasova, 2015; Coxhead, 2000; Nation, 2001, 2006). The GSL can be accessed at http://jbauman.com/gsl.html.

Perhaps one of the first word lists that targeted academic language was the American University Word List which was written by Jean Praninskas in 1972 while she was Director of the University Orientation Program at the American University of Beirut. This list included 507 base words and 840 derived forms of the base words. In this very early example of EAP corpus research, Praninskas created a corpus from ten textbooks used in freshman classes in the fields of math, chemistry, biology, physics, psychology, sociology, history, and English rhetoric and literature. In her methodology, Praninskas sampled words—without computer assistance—from every tenth page of these books, which produced a corpus of approximately 270,000 words, a number that is woefully small compared to corpora today with well over 500 million words (e.g., Corpus of Contemporary American English or COCA), but yet much bigger than anyone had done for EAP at that time. As a researcher who was also a teacher, Praninskas started with a practical research question: "Which words do my university students need to know to be able to read their coursebooks?" She then created an appropriate corpus—from actual coursebooks—and identified the words that would appear in her list. In 1972, this methodology was then considered and still remains a remarkable milestone.

A subsequent EAP list was the University Word List (UWL) (Xue & Nation, 1984). In their methodology, the researchers decided to exclude the first 2,000 words of the GSL because students should already know these words before moving to academic language. The UWL included 836 words grouped in 11 levels, with Level 1 having more frequent words than Level 11. According to Nation (1990), these 836 words account for 8 percent of the words in a typical text. The UWL can be accessed at http://jbauman.com/UWL.html.

The Natural Approach Fades

The AWL has become perhaps the most widely used vocabulary list in text-books and curricula for students in academic settings, especially EAP courses, as these learners work to improve their English proficiency (Banister, 2016; O'Sullivan, 2007; Paquot, 2007). To be sure, there are other good academic word lists today, but the AWL is one that many teachers are familiar with. When Averil Coxhead (2000) published the AWL in a very influential article in *TESOL Quarterly* in 2000, she had no idea this list would end up having the massive impact it has had on language education. In fact, writing about the AWL a full decade after it was published, Coxhead (2011) summed up her sincere surprise by saying, "I can honestly say that the AWL has had a far greater and more international impact than I ever imagined [when I was doing my thesis work] back in 1998" (p. 360).

Just a decade or so before the AWL was published, the popularity of such a word list in L2 education might have been unfathomable. The Natural Approach was still our main theoretical framework, and learning from a word list was not considered natural. However, by the mid-1990s, educators had begun to seriously question the effectiveness of the Natural Approach (Atkinson, 1993; Lightbown & Pienemann, 1993). As it turns out, language programs using the Natural Approach for a decade or more had not experienced the markedly improved success rates for their ESL or EFL students (or for that matter, Spanish or French or other foreign language learners in high schools and university programs either) that proponents of the Natural Approach had envisioned.

The label "natural" may have a positive connotation, but how natural a task is in L1 acquisition may have little to no bearing on its effectiveness in an L2 classroom for learners or teachers. Many learners, especially secondary students and adults, reported they were dissatisfied with their courses using the Natural Approach because they wanted more explicit attention to form—that is, more grammar instruction and more error correction (Azar, 2007; Havranek, 2002; Katayama, 2007; Yoshida, 2008; Zhou, 2009). Leading journals began to publish empirical research studies (e.g., Doughty, 1991), showing that classroom instruction that included focus on language, especially grammar, was in fact effective, which suddenly not only allowed but actually encouraged teachers to explicitly teach grammar or correct students' errors again. In sum, a major paradigm shift had occurred, with teachers no longer confined or relegated to the role of providing input for language acquisition.

An Explosive Growth of Interest in L2 Vocabulary Research

In the late 1990s, there was perhaps coincidentally a mini-explosion of L2 vocabulary research published in leading journals. This research offered a huge number of interesting studies on L2 vocabulary with practical implications for teachers of different languages. For example, some of these early influential studies were not limited to just ESL/EFL learners but also of Dutch as a Second Language (Hulstijn, 1992) and French as a Foreign Language (Hulstijn et al., 1996).

In 2011, Paul Nation, a major leader in promoting the importance of vocabulary teaching and research, astutely summed up this spike in lexical interest when he noted that more than 30 percent of the research on L1 and L2 vocabulary learning in the last 120 years had actually been published in just 12 years: 1999–2011. What contributed to this sudden upsurge? One could quite convincingly argue the publication of the AWL research in 2000 was the single biggest catalyst that sparked teacher interest in vocabulary in English language teaching, which in turn encouraged more researcher interest. Teachers recognized that the AWL was a practical teaching tool based on actual research that they could understand: the words came from a large corpus of real language, not one person's mere intuitions.

Since then, L2 research articles have been published on an incredibly wide range of L2 vocabulary topics, including how many words L2 learners need to know (again, along the lines of Coxhead 2000), how L2 learners' vocabularies develop, why some words are more difficult to learn than others, whether L2 vocabulary is learned more easily through natural context or through direct instruction (such as with a list), which vocabulary learning strategies successful students tend to employ, and which types of written practice exercises promote vocabulary learning.

Enter the AWL

The need for focused vocabulary lists had therefore been established, and the groundwork using valid corpus methodology had been laid. In the mid-1990s, Averil Coxhead set out to improve on the UWL and produce a better list of academic vocabulary for ESL learners, which she eventually published as the AWL in 2000. Since that time, her Academic Word List has been freely available at https://www.victoria.ac.nz/lals/resources/academicwordlist.

Coxhead (2018, pp. 3–4) explained her early research planning for the AWL:

> During my postgraduate studies back in Aotearoa/New Zealand, I began to teach EAP. It was during this time that I became more aware of research in vocabulary studies and how it could inform and, in some cases, transform the learning and teaching objectives of a class. I consulted Jim Dickie at Victoria University, a wise lecturer in my postgraduate studies, about doing a thesis as part of my master's study. Jim said, 'You know what works, but you don't know why.' This was another turning point. And then John Read, also then at Victoria University, mentioned that Xue and Nation's (1984) University Word List needed updating. So I went to talk to Paul Nation. This is how the Academic Word List (AWL) (Coxhead, 2000) research began. I have been lucky enough to be able to have opportunities to talk about research with these and other great colleagues in Aotearoa/New Zealand and in far-flung places many times over the last 20 years.

The AWL did not take off right away, but it is doubtful that any type of word list would have been well received at this time, given the lingering mindset of the Natural Approach. In the mid-1990s, when I presented TESOL conference workshops on using word lists to teach vocabulary, the audience sizes were usually small. Still influenced by the Natural Approach, teachers questioned the wisdom of using a word list instead of letting students acquire vocabulary naturally through reading or listening. Right around the time when the AWL first came out, vocabulary sessions started to appear more often on conference programs, and today almost every TESOL conference features multiple presentations and workshops on teaching vocabulary. Teachers are no longer asking if they should present academic vocabulary, but rather *how* they should best do so. In response, many publishers of academic ESL (or EAP) materials now publish textbooks featuring AWL vocabulary and a variety of practice activities for those words.

The Real Impact of the AWL on English Language Teaching and Research

While the AWL can certainly be a valuable classroom tool, its real impact in our field is much more than the mere compilation of the 570 word families. The reason that Coxhead's AWL was in fact revolutionary in the field of TESOL was that it drew massive teacher attention to the lexical needs of our students while at the same time offering teachers and learners a practical solution, one that was scientifically based—that is, from a corpus instead of just human intuition. The AWL led to the development of other word lists based on actual learner needs to help them succeed in their academic work, which in turn led to even more research on second language vocabulary teaching and learning.

4. Which Words Are on the AWL?

This should be an easy question to answer, but in fact there are at least four ways to list the words, each providing a different set of words.

Headwords and Inflected Forms

The AWL consists of 570 word families, which translates to 3,111 (Hartshorn & Hart, 2016) or 3,112 (Hyland & Tse, 2007) words. A **word family** consists of a **headword**, which is the main word in a word family (usually a stem noun or verb form) along with forms with inflections and frequent prefixes and suffixes. For example, the word family for the headword *significant* might also include eight other words: *insignificant, insignificantly, significance, significantly, signified, signifies, signify, signifying.*

Why Coxhead Used Word Families

Why should we base the AWL on word families and not just words? Considering research conducted before 2000, Coxhead concluded that if students learned word roots along with common inflections, they might be able to learn words that are related to each other (Hernandez, 2017). In fact, her decision to use the word family and not the word is "controversial" (Coxhead, 2011), as well as a frequent criticism of the AWL. (Other lists such as the Academic Vocabulary List [Gardner & Davies, 2014] instead consist of individual words called "lemmas," which is explained in more depth in Chapter 6, "How Do Other Word Lists Differ from the AWL?".)

Organization of the AWL

The 570 word families of the AWL are arranged in ten sublists to facilitate student use. Sublists 1 through 9 contain 60 words, while Sublist 10 contains only 30 words. These sublists represent the frequency of occurrence of the words in academic language, so the words in Sublist 1 occur more frequently than the words in Sublist 2, which are in turn much more frequent than the words in Sublist 10.

Four Ways to Present the AWL Words

Different sites present the AWL in different arrangements, including at least four options as seen in the pages that follow. It is important to understand these four options so you can recommend the best one for your learners. The complete AWL can be found online in several places, including https://www. victoria.ac.nz/lals/resources/academicwordlist.

Option 1: Alphabetically by Headword

Some people prefer a list of all 570 headwords in alphabetical order:

abandon, abstract, academy, access, accommodate, accompany, accumulate, accurate, achieve, acknowledge, acquire, adapt, adequate, adjacent, adjust, administration, adult, advocate, affect, aggregate, aid, albeit, allocate, alter, alternative, ambiguous, amend, analogy, analyze, annual, anticipate, apparent, append, appreciate, approach, appropriate, approximate, arbitrary, area, aspect, assemble, assess, assign, assist, assume, assure, attach, attain, attitude, attribute, author, authority, automate, available, aware, behalf, benefit, bias, bond, brief, bulk, capable, capacity, category, cease, challenge, channel, chapter, chart, chemical, circumstance, cite, civil, clarify, classic, clause, code, coherent, coincide, collapse, colleague, commence, comment, commission, commit, commodity, communicate, community, compatible, compensate, compile, complement, complex, component, compound, comprehensive, comprise, compute, conceive, concentrate, concept, conclude, concurrent, conduct, confer, confine, confirm, conflict, conform, consent, consequent, considerable, consist, constant, constitute, constrain, construct, consult, consume, contact, contemporary, context, contract, contradict, contrary, contrast, contribute, controversy, convene, converse, convert, convince, cooperate, coordinate, core, corporate, correspond, couple, create, credit, criteria, crucial, culture, currency, cycle, data, debate, decade, decline, deduce, define, definite, demonstrate, denote, deny, depress, derive, design, despite, detect, deviate, device, devote, differentiate, dimension, diminish, discrete, discriminate, displace, display, dispose, distinct, distort, distribute, diverse, document, domain, domestic, dominate, draft, drama, duration, dynamic, economy, edit, element, eliminate, emerge, emphasis, empirical, enable, encounter, energy, enforce, enhance, enormous, ensure, entity, environment, equate, equip, equivalent, erode, error, establish, estate, estimate, ethic, ethnic, evaluate, eventual, evident, evolve, exceed, exclude, exhibit, expand, expert, explicit, exploit, export, expose, external, extract, facilitate, factor, feature, federal, fee, file, final, finance, finite, flexible, fluctuate, focus, format, formula, forthcoming, found, foundation, framework, function, fund, fundamental, furthermore, gender, generate, generation, globe, goal, grade, grant, guarantee, guideline, hence, hierarchy, highlight, hypothesis, identical, identify, ideology, ignorance, illustrate, image, immigrate, impact, implement, implicate, implicit, imply, impose, incentive, incidence, incline, income, incorporate, index, indicate, individual, induce, inevitable, infer, infrastructure, inherent, inhibit, initial, initiate, injure, innovate, input, insert, insight, inspect, instance, institute, instruct, integral, integrate, integrity, intelligence, intense, interact, intermediate, internal, interpret, interval, intervene, intrinsic, invest, investigate, invoke, involve, isolate, issue, item, job, journal, justify, label, labor, layer, lecture, legal, legislate, levy, liberal, license, likewise, link, locate, logic, maintain, major, manipulate, manual, margin, mature, maximize, mechanism, media, mediate, medical, medium, mental, method, migrate, military, minimal, minimize, minimum, ministry, minor, mode, modify, monitor, motive, mutual, negate, network, neutral, nevertheless, nonetheless, norm, normal, notion, notwithstanding, nuclear, objective, obtain, obvious, occupy, occur, odd, offset, ongoing, option, orient, outcome, output, overall, overlap, overseas, panel, paradigm, paragraph, parallel, parameter, participate, partner, passive, perceive, percent, period, persist, perspective, phase, phenomenon, philosophy, physical, plus, policy, portion, pose, positive, potential, practitioner, precede, precise, predict, predominant, preliminary, presume, previous, primary, prime, principal, principle, prior, priority, proceed, process, professional, prohibit, project, promote, proportion, prospect, protocol, psychology, publication, publish, purchase, pursue, qualitative, quote, radical, random, range, ratio, rational, react, recover, refine, regime, region, register, regulate, reinforce, reject, relax, release, relevant, reluctance, rely, remove, require, research, reside, resolve, resource, respond, restore, restrain, restrict, retain, reveal, revenue, reverse, revise, revolution, rigid, role, route, scenario, schedule, scheme, scope, section, sector, secure, seek, select, sequence, series, sex, shift, significant, similar, simulate, site, so-called, sole, somewhat, source, specific, specify, sphere, stable, statistic, status, straightforward, strategy, stress, structure, style, submit, subordinate, subsequent, subsidy, substitute, successor, sufficient, sum, summary, supplement, survey, survive, suspend, sustain, symbol, tape, target, task, team, technical, technique, technology, temporary, tense, terminate, text, theme, theory, thereby, thesis, topic, trace, tradition, transfer, transform, transit, transmit, transport, trend, trigger, ultimate, undergo, underlie, undertake, uniform, unify, unique, utilize, valid, vary, vehicle, version, via, violate, virtual, visible, vision, visual, volume, voluntary, welfare, whereas, whereby, widespread

Option 2: Alphabetically by Headword with Word Family Members

Some prefer the headword and all family members, as seen for the first two words from Sublist 1:

- analyze—analytically, analytical, analyzing, analyzing, analyzers, analyzes, analyzed, analytic, analysts, analysis, analyses, analyzer, analyst
- approach—unapproachable, approachable, approaching, approaches, approached

Option 3: Alphabetically by Headword with Word Family Members and the Most Frequent Word Italicized

This arrangement makes it easier to focus on the most frequent word, which is the one most worth learning. Sometimes the most frequent word is not the headword, as seen with *analysis*:

- analyze—analytically, analytical, analyzing, analyzing, analyzers, analyzes, analyzed, analytic, analysts, *analysis*, analyses, analyzer, analyst
- approach—unapproachable, *approachable*, approaching, approaches, approached

Option 4: Only the Most Frequent Member of Each Word Family by Sublists

My personal favorite as a learner would be this list of only the most frequent members of each word family. To me, this is the most beneficial to a learner who is short on time and needs the words that are actually frequent (and not the whole word family).

- analysis
- approach

How Should I Present the AWL Words to My Students?

Of these four options, which should teachers and students use? There is no one correct way to organize the AWL, so teachers should use the option that matches their students' English needs.

Keeping in mind that the goal of any vocabulary list is to help students learn the most frequently used words quickly, here are my recommendations:

- Option 1 is not particularly helpful because students will learn only one form for each family—that is, the headword—but that form might not even be the most common form.
- Option 2 resembles a dictionary. It is an alphabetical listing of all the words in a word family without any consideration of frequency. Giving students 16 forms (as in the case of *analyze*) when we know that many of their forms are not at all frequent goes against the whole purpose of a useful corpus-based word list. I strongly believe that we should not teach a word form just because it exists linguistically. In sum, if it is not a word form that you can imagine your students actually needing, then please do not teach it because that word form does not meet your learners' needs.
- Option 3 lists all the word as in Option 2, but is slightly better in that indicates the most common word form (in italics).
- Option 4 is the best by far. It lists the 570 most frequent words in Coxhead's academic corpus.

Perhaps the single biggest mistake I have seen with the AWL occurs when teachers and textbooks try to teach suffixes (and some prefixes) using the AWL. Options 2 and 3 are great for this, but this was never the purpose of the AWL. The AWL deals with vocabulary, not grammar. I find it ludicrous to build a list to make learning vocabulary easier by identifying the most common words and then have students attempt to learn word families, thereby increasing the learning burden when research tells us that many of those word family members are not frequent. Laufer and Cobb (2019), for example, found that a reader could reach the important 95 percent coverage of words on a page of academic text without knowing most of the derived words in a word family.

For me, the main purpose of a vocabulary list is to speed up the language learning process by giving the students the English words they will need for listening, writing, reading, or speaking. ESL students do not have a lot of time, so we need a list that makes learning efficient. Why would we give students a list of words that may not be the most frequent form (Option 1), or all the words in the word family (Options 2 and 3)? Given our students' lack of time and weak vocabulary knowledge, I think Option 4 is the best presentation to give students and the best list for teachers to use in planning lessons.

Teachers should also realize that students are not aware of the four presentations of the AWL, so you may wish to explain this briefly to your students so they can choose wisely. My students are often very eager to do online practices with the AWL, so I try to help my students determine whether a website practices the headword (Option 1), the entire word family (Options 2 and 3), or just the most frequent word in the family (Option 4).

5. How Were the 570 Word Families of the AWL Selected?

A subtitle for this section might be "How complex is the process by which any corpus-based lists is compiled?" Using an appropriate corpus and valid research methodology can be a huge, complex, and time-consuming undertaking, but it will produce a list that is more accurate than what any individual can produce based on intuition alone.

The Science Behind Creating Word Lists from a Corpus

For some readers, this section may seem too detailed because here I explain how Coxhead compiled the AWL. However, because any word list is only as strong as how carefully it was compiled, it is important for teachers to understand the methodology behind the AWL and other corpus-based lists.

Coxhead's Three Steps

Coxhead completed three important steps to produce the final Academic Word List. For each of the steps she took, the field provided very little existing corpus research that could inform her of how to proceed with the undertaking of such an enormous academic task. What may appear as easy or obvious to us now was not so clear in the late 1990s when she was doing her groundbreaking work.

Step 1: Create a Corpus

Compiling a corpus gives list makers the data they need to determine the most frequent words. In addition, a corpus can allow us to see how a word or phrase is actually used in real language, as opposed to our intuition of how we think it is used or how it should be used because we were taught to say a certain phrase a certain way.

For most teachers, using a corpus may seem foreign, but teachers use corpus linguistics all the time without ever realizing it. Students frequently ask teachers questions about the usage of a language point such as "What is the difference between *make* and *do?*" or "Do *convince* and *persuade* have the same meaning?" When teachers attempt to answer these questions in class, the teachers are not consulting a book or Google. Instead, the teachers are asking themselves what they think the answer is, based on all the information and experiences that are stored in their head at that moment. In other words, they are doing a corpus search, and their "corpus" consists of everything stored in their brain up to that moment. This Q&A is normal, but any one teacher's answers are biased because they are based on only one person's set of experiences. Worse, it is what the person *thinks* is happening in English—that is, their opinion—and not necessarily what is a fact. A large corpus allows us to find out the facts about how a word is used, not just how we think it might be used.

People create a corpus for a specific goal, and within TESOL, one goal might be to identify the language used in academic settings so that teachers can design better lessons and materials to help students succeed in their high school or university classes. The Michigan Corpus of Academic Spoken English (MICASE) is a collection of 1.8 million words of transcribed speech from a wide array of speech events, including lectures, class discussions, lab meetings, and office hours from the University of Michigan. It is freely searchable at https://quod.lib.umich.edu/m/micase/. Though the corpus is a bit dated, I think it is still valuable because of the variety of types of interactions. As expected, it has academic lectures on several topics from different courses, but I believe that the transcripts of the study groups are representative of natural university student speech in informal settings.

One of the most widely used corpora in TESOL today is the Corpus of Contemporary American English (COCA). According to https://corpus.byu.edu/coca/, this corpus is "the largest freely-available corpus of English and the only large and balanced corpus of American English." It consists of more than 600 million words of text that were taken equally from spoken interactions, fiction, popular magazines, and academic texts. Furthermore, this corpus allows a chronological search of word occurrence, since there are 20 million words from each year between 1990 and 2019.

When Coxhead started her research in the late 1990s, her original goal was to assemble a corpus of 4 million words. However, due to logistical limitations, she ended up using a corpus of just over 3.5 million words.

Why this size? Earlier on, a decision had been made that for a word to be included in the resulting AWL, it had to occur at least 100 times in the corpus. In order to identify a word family with 100 occurrences, Coxhead (2000) knew from earlier research using the Brown Corpus (Francis & Kucera, 1982) that she needed a corpus as large as 3.5 million words, so it was thought that a corpus of at least 3.5 million words would be sufficient to allow an analysis to identify words that might occur at least 100 times.

How large does a corpus need to be? Well, it depends on what you are analyzing and how the results will be used. To be successful, the analysis will have to have a large enough number of occurrences of the word for us to identify the patterns of its usage. Reppen (2010) provides an outstanding overview of how to build a corpus, including information on size and text collection. For example, consider the word *of*. It is the fourth most common word in COCA. In the 600 million total words in COCA, the word *of* occurs 15,778,596 times, meaning that it occurs approximately 2.6 times every 100 words, or roughly once every 38 words. In a corpus of 100,000 words, therefore, we might expect to find 2,600 examples. This number of occurrences is a very healthy sample size to analyze so we can have an idea of how this word behaves in English. For example, is *of* usually followed by a noun (*the quality of books*) or a pronoun (*of them*)? How often is followed by a gerund (*instead of going*)? How often is it preceded by an adjective (e.g., *tired of hearing that*)?

While Coxhead's corpus of 3.5 million words may not seem very large today, especially when compared with COCA's 600 million words, her corpus has proved to be of sufficient size for what she was trying to accomplish, namely compiling a representative list of the most frequently used vocabulary in her academic corpus.

Step 2: Operationalize (Define) a "Word"

Coxhead's next step was to select the words, but this is not as easy as it might initially seem. What exactly is a *word*? While we might think we know what a word is, the question becomes a lot more complex and much more important when trying to identify specific vocabulary.

In every study, researchers must set certain, often arbitrary, limitations to specify, or operationalize, what a given item is—and, just as importantly, what it is not. For vocabulary researchers, the most basic yet perplexing issue is determining a "word."

Are *go* and *goes* the same word? The suffix is different, but the meanings are exactly the same. What about *went*? It looks like a different word, but it is just the past tense of the same meaning. If *go* and *goes* count as the same word, then what about *is* and *are*? What about contractions like *it's* and *it is*? Should *it's* meaning "it is" and *it's* meaning "it has" count as separate words? What about idioms such as *out of the blue* or *all at once*, or phrases such as *in spite of*, or lexical bundles such as *one of the most*?

We need to consider what we will count, and perhaps the most basic question is whether to count words or word families. Obviously focusing on words versus word families will produce very different lists in the end.

For some people, using word families seems normal because—in theory— the words have the same or similar meanings. However, is this always true?

Most people would agree that *goal* and *goals* are the same word because the second noun *goals* has the same meaning as the first noun *goal* though the form of the word is different (singular vs. plural).

What about when the part of speech changes? Would you say that the adjective *consistent* is the same word as the adverb *consistently*? Many people would answer yes because the meaning is still the same, but what about the noun *consistency*? This is more complicated perhaps because *consistency* is **polysemous**.

Consider these examples of the word *consistency*:

A. *An employee with Martha's <u>consistency</u> of service deserves a promotion.*
B. *Some people do not like the <u>consistency</u> of mayonnaise.*

Yes, Example B is a completely different topic, and the meaning of *consistency* here is not the same as in Example A. Does this make it a different word?

Native speakers are aware of the challenges of polysemy. For example, when I ask native speaker teachers what the word *take* means, many move their hand miming someone grabbing or picking up something, and this certainly is one possible meaning. However, I will bet you can think of many other meanings of the word *take*. In English, we can also (1) *take* something to someone, (2) *take* notes, (3) *take* a shower, (4) *take* a bus, (5) *take* medicine, and (6) *take* a nap. In fact, Merriam Webster's definition of the verb *take* lists 85 meanings with an additional 47 special expressions such as *take into account* and *take care of*, which can also be referred to as lexical bundles.

Recognizing that vocabulary is more than just single words, many corpus researchers insist that multi-word vocabulary items are crucial to overall language proficiency. **Lexical bundles**, which are two or more words that occur together with high frequency but are not idiomatic, must be part of good academic word lists (Byrd & Coxhead, 2010). In a detailed examination of lexical bundles in university teaching and textbooks, Biber and colleagues (2004) give examples to prove that lexical bundles are the building blocks of discourse, as seen later in Hyland's 2012 research. Simpson-Vlach and Ellis (2010) produced the Academic Formulas List using a very rigorous set of criteria for inclusion. Paquot and Granger (2012) demonstrated the need for learners to receive more systematic instruction in formulaic language. For an outstanding review of research on lexical bundles by students, see Mbodj and Crossley (2020).

Step 3: Decide Which Words Are Academic

The AWL has academic words, but how do you know if a word is academic or not? Unfortunately, there is no standard definition.

Most people assume that a word was included in the AWL because of its frequency in the academic corpus, but if frequency were the sole criterion, the AWL would include *the* because it is the most common word in English. In fact, Coxhead had three guiding principles in determining whether to include or exclude a word from the final list of 570 word families:

1. Outside the GSL: One of the assumptions made was that learners interested in studying more specialized vocabulary such as that found in the AWL would have mastered the basic words in the General Service List, so GSL words, no matter how frequent in the academic corpus, were excluded from the AWL.
2. Frequency: Only words that occurred at least 100 times within the 3.5-million-word corpus were considered for the AWL.
3. Range: The list should represent general academic material, so the list should consist of words common in many academic fields, not just one or two. Coxhead decided a word had to occur at least 10 times in each of the four main sections (arts, commerce, law, science) and in at least 15 of the 28 subject areas (i.e., more than half of the subject areas).

A Blueprint for Other Lists

The AWL has now become the standard for creating corpus-based lists. Whenever a new list is published, the article introducing it to the TESOL educational community always has a very detailed methods section in which the authors of the new list explain how their list is different from the AWL and then mention what is similar. Everything revolves around the AWL.

In addition to the creation of a unique word list, Coxhead has had a much wider impact on English language education in general. I would argue the AWL was the single most influential catalyst in our field that helped ignite a flourishing interest in vocabulary, certainly among teachers who recognize the need for attention to vocabulary in all language classes, but also among researchers who strive to develop better vocabulary word lists based on sound methodology using real language sources instead of intuition.

Potential Limitations of the AWL

While the AWL has many supporters, there is also criticism of certain aspects of Coxhead's methodology, usually centering on three main issues. First, Minshall (2013) notes the AWL corpus seems to favor some disciplines over others, especially business. Second, Gardner and Davies (2014) and others strongly object to the use of the word family as the unit of counting. Finally, Hyland and Tse (2007) and Durrant (2014) have demonstrated that vocabulary use differs across disciplines. Hyland and Tse (2007) go so far as to question the existence of "general academic vocabulary," instead arguing for more discipline-specific vocabulary lists, something that future research should definitely consider. Ultimately, that is the solution for those who object to Coxhead's methodology: create your own methodology, explain and support your decisions, develop a new list, and empirically demonstrate its superiority.

I would also add another under-discussed factor in the creation of the AWL: students' native language. The AWL was developed in New Zealand, which has a very different ESL population from the U.S., where I live. According to a fellow materials writer who worked with New Zealand high school ESL students, most of her students came from Tonga, Samoa, and China (L. Horvath, personal communication, January 4, 2020). Though just one anecdote, these languages are in stark contrast to the situation in the U.S., where about 77 percent of limited English proficiency students in K–12 classes speak Spanish at home.

Spanish and English vocabularies have much more in common than Chinese and English vocabularies do. Using a very stringent set of guidelines to identify how many AWL words are cognates for Spanish-speaking students, Bushong (2010) found that 76 percent (434 words) of the AWL words are true cognates, with the remainder being partial cognates (14 words or 2 percent), false cognates (16 words or 3 percent), and non-cognates (106 words or 19 percent). Teachers with learners whose first language is Spanish (or another Romance language such as Portuguese, French, Italian, or Romanian) should be aware that the learning burden of the different AWL words is not the same. For some secondary Spanish-speaking students, these words may not be as much of an issue because of the high number of true cognates. As Bushong (2010, p. 3) aptly explains the problem:

> One of the shortcomings of word lists is that they are designed for ELLs of all L1 backgrounds. This shortcoming was observed as far back as 1957 when, in reference to two influential English word lists, Lado stated that "we simply cannot ignore the native language of the student as a factor of primary importance in vocabulary" (p. 81). He was referring specifically to the fact that there exist a high number of English-Spanish cognate pairs in the English language and that word lists should take this important fact into account. Explicit focus on cognates eases the "learning burden of a word" (Nation, 1990, p. 33). Since the word is similar in form and meaning in both English and Spanish, SSELLs [Spanish-speaking English Language Learners] expend less effort in the learning of those words than they would non-cognates. Therefore ... awareness of English-Spanish cognates on the AWL would assist in SSELLs' learning of English academic vocabulary.

If Coxhead's usual ESL classes had consisted largely of Romance language speakers such as Spanish, would she have been as inclined to allow the inclusion of so many Spanish-English cognates into the AWL?

Having read all of this information, perhaps you now have a new appreciation of how complicated the process of compiling a corpus-based list can be. This meticulous attention to these steps, however, produces a vocabulary list that more accurately reflects students' real L2 needs. For further reading, Nation's (2016) *Making and Using Word Lists for Language Learning and Testing* is an excellent resource.

6. How Do Other Word Lists Differ from the AWL?

When Coxhead's (2000) AWL first appeared in *TESOL Quarterly* in 2000, only a very few corpus-based word lists existed. Since then, other researchers have identified limitations of the AWL and used Coxhead's basic methodology to produce dozens of corpus-based lists for many different purposes, including general communication, academic work, and specific disciplines. In an excellent overview of lists, Lessard-Clouston (2012–13) discusses two lists of English formulaic expressions and several subject-specific English word lists in fields varying from agriculture, business, and engineering to medicine and theology. Similarly, Youngblood and Folse (2017) highlight 31 corpus-based lists grouped into four categories (general, academic, disciplinary, formulaic).

Despite the abundance of existing corpus-based lists, each year sees the publication of even more such lists. Speaking about this explosion of corpus-based word lists, D. Schmitt (2016) cautions the field to evaluate lists very closely according to an array of factors, considering especially the real purpose of the list, the corpus on which it is based (Miller & Biber, 2015), and what counts as a *word*.

34 Corpus-Based Academic Word Lists

In alphabetical order, here are 34 of the many corpus-based word lists currently available for English for Academic Purposes (EAP):

1. Academic Articles Word List for Social Sciences (Kwary & Artha, 2017)
2. Academic Collocation List (ACL) (Ackermann & Chen, 2013)
3. Academic Keyword List (AKL) (Paquot, 2010)
4. Academic Formulas List (AFL) (Simpson-Vlach & N. Ellis, 2010)
5. Academic Spoken Vocabulary in TED Talks List (Liu & Chen, 2019)
6. Academic Spoken Word List (Dang et al., 2017)
7. Academic Vocabulary List (AVL) (Gardner & Davies, 2014)
8. Academic Word List (AWL) (Coxhead, 2000)

9. Academic Word List for Applied Linguistics Research Articles (Khani & Tazik, 2013)
10. AgroCorpus List (Martínez et al., 2009)
11. Basic Engineering List (BEL) (Ward, 2009)
12. Business Word List (BWL) (Konstantakis, 2007)
13. Business Word List (BWL) (Hsu, 2011)
14. Chemistry Academic Word List (Valipouri & Nassaji, 2013)
15. Computer Science Word List (Minshall, 2013)
16. Economics Academic Word List (EAWL) (O'Flynn, 2019)
17. Environmental Academic Word List (Liu & Han, 2015)
18. Hard Science Spoken Word List (Dang, 2018)
19. Medical Academic Word List (MAWL) (Wang et al., 2008)
20. Medical Word List (Hsu, 2013)
21. Middle School Vocabulary Lists (Greene & Coxhead, 2015)
22. New Academic Word List (NAWL) (Browne et al., 2013a)
23. New General Service List (NGSL) (Browne et al., 2013b)
24. New General Service List (NGSL) (Brezina & Gablasova, 2015)
25. New Medical Academic Word List (Lei & Liu, 2016)
26. Nursing Academic Word List (Yang, 2014)
27. Opaque Engineering Word List (Watson-Todd, 2017)
28. Oxford Phrasal Academic Lexicon (OPAL) (2020) https://www.oxfordlearnersdictionaries.com/us/wordlists/opal
29. Phrasal Expressions List (PHRASE List) (Martinez & Schmitt, 2012)
30. Pilot Science Word List for EAP (Coxhead & Hirsh, 2007)
31. Psychology Word List (Safari, 2018)
32. Spoken Academic Word List (Nesi, 2002)
33. Theological Word List (Lessard-Clouston, 2010)
34. Test of English for International Communication List (TOEIC) (Browne & Culligan, 2020)

As you can see from this substantial list, there are in fact many EAP word lists that are based on a corpus, which is clearly a major improvement over where we were prior to when the AWL came out in 2000. Amazingly, all of these lists were developed within just two decades. Of the 34 lists, 79 percent were published within the last 10 years. Therefore, even though vocabulary teaching has long been a core part of language training, corpus-based lists are still in their infancy, relatively speaking.

The Coxhead (2000), which is the oldest of these EAP lists, has become the standard. However, each of these other lists was produced because that list's creator perceived some limitation in the AWL and sought to improve upon it. In fact, the methodology section of any corpus-based list certainly mentions Coxhead (2000) and how the new list differs from the AWL.

With so many lists, a teacher's question now must be "Which one is the best?" My answer is "It depends." To help you figure out which list is better suited for your students and/or your teaching style, I will focus on the four key aspects of what I believe that a good corpus-based EAP list should have: (1) appropriate corpus, (2) suitable methodology, (3) useful unit of counting, and (4) high coverage, including not just overall frequency but wider use throughout the corpus.

An Appropriate Corpus

A good list, especially with today's modern computer technology, should be based on a corpus, not people's intuitions or experience. Today, no one should be using vocabulary lists that do not have a corpus basis. Pure intuition is out, use of corpus data is in.

In order for a corpus to produce a list that accurately reflects the array of vocabulary used, that corpus should be of a substantial size. Coxhead's corpus for the AWL included 3.5 million words, which in 2000 was considered quite a feat. However, today's faster and more powerful computers allow much easier processing of large corpora, so subsequent lists have used corpora with many more words. For example, the corpus for the Academic Spoken Word List (Dang et al., 2017) has 13 million words, the Academic Vocabulary List (Gardner & Davies, 2014) comes from a corpus of 120 million words, and the New Academic Word List (Browne et al., 2013a) was compiled from a corpus of 288 million words.

We should also be careful of the academic skill associated with a corpus. We should not assume that a corpus based on textbooks that students are to read will give us the type of vocabulary normally used in student essays or other written assignments (Durrant, 2016), or vice versa. If students want to master the academic vocabulary needed to write an essay for a content class, then they need a vocabulary list compiled from a corpus of quality papers written by students in that same content class.

Why have we almost blindly assumed that there is a one-size-fits-all type of academic word list suitable for all skills? For example, how does the language spoken by the professor in a lecture class compare with the language used in the textbook for the same class? Dang and colleagues (2017) point out that the coverage of AWL words in text is roughly 10 percent, but only 4 percent in academic speech. The academic vocabulary needs for these two modalities is vastly different. As a result, a corpus that is based on high school textbooks would be suitable to compile a word list that might help high school students master the vocabulary they need to read a high school textbook, while a word list based on a corpus of lectures from a history course might help students with the vocabulary necessary to comprehend history lectures.

A good list for your students should be based on a corpus that includes materials that also match the academic program level of your students as much as possible. If a corpus includes textbooks, for instance, those textbooks should match your students' academic program level. Undergraduate university students need language for undergraduate textbooks, not high school or graduate school materials, and definitely not academic journals. While the academic vocabulary in a high school textbook may be very similar to the academic vocabulary in a university textbook or even in an article from a history journal, we do not know this, and it should not be taken for granted. (This area is wide open to researchers seeking to improve our understanding of academic language.)

Be especially wary of lists based on corpora that include a substantial percentage of academic journal articles—unless you are training students to write an academic journal article, which is almost never the case. Based on conversations I have had with my own undergraduate students, very few of them have to read an academic article for any of their classes. Those who do report having to read an academic article tell me they may have to read only one or at most two per semester. Instead, their class reading material consists of their textbook, a few handouts from the professor, discussion posts in an online discussion board, and maybe some websites. While graduate students may have to read articles from time to time, we can fairly safely assume that most of them are not trying to write an academic journal article for publication. For this reason, students should not be overly encouraged to write using vocabulary that comes from a corpus of journal articles. There is little proof that this type of corpus matches our undergraduate students' writing goals.

Why then are several of the 34 lists based partially or wholly on academic journal articles? The answer is simple: convenience. It is very easy to retrieve 500,000 words of text from academic journal articles from the internet. However, this is not a genre that many students need to emulate and is therefore a bad practice in general.

An excellent example of compiling a corpus that carefully matches student needs, not just convenience of obtaining materials, is the Academic

Spoken Word List (Dang et al., 2017). The authors chose materials that "represented (as closely as possible) the academic speech that EAP learners from a wide range of academic disciplines are likely to encounter in their academic study in English-medium programs" (p. 968). Further underscoring their goal of assembling a corpus that matched actual student needs, the authors used four different types of speech events common to the university student experience: lectures, seminars, labs, and tutorials.

Before you accept a word list as a good fit for your students, learn more about the corpus that was used to produce that list. A word list designed to help university students write essays and assignments in their first college year should not be assumed good if it is based on a corpus composed of newspapers, training manuals, or articles from professional journals.

Methodology

As shown in the discussion of the detailed methodology behind the Academic Word List (Coxhead, 2000), determining which words to include in a final vocabulary list requires many complex steps. This careful attention to detail certainly helps to produce a valid and useful academic list in the end. Newer lists may differ from the AWL in two important ways: reliance on other lists and minimum frequency.

Even though a word is very frequent in a corpus, some list makers may automatically exclude the word just because it already appears on another list, usually one that is deemed easier. For example, when Coxhead (2000) compiled the AWL, she made a decision to exclude any of the words in the GSL (West, 1953) from her AWL, because it was assumed that students ready to learn academic words would have already mastered the more frequent general vocabulary in the GSL. Because the AWL is seen as the standard bearer of modern corpus-based lists, subsequent lists often tried to emulate Coxhead's methodology.

One criticism of this type of exclusion is that some GSL words are in fact also frequent in academic language where they sometimes have a different meaning. For instance, the word *while* is among the 2,000 frequent words in the GSL, so Coxhead automatically excluded it from the AWL. This is problematic for English learners because *while* is used differently in academic writing than in conversation. In conversation, *while* usually refers to a simultaneous action (*While I was cooking dinner, Chris was watching TV*), but in academic writing, *while* is more commonly used to express contrast (*While a majority of voters approved the amendment in 2015, the vote was not the predicted landslide.*) Students are much more likely to know the conversation meaning of *while* but not its academic meaning, so including *while* in an academic word list—*with its academic meaning*—would seem the correct thing to do.

A second difference between the AWL and other lists is how frequently a word had to occur in the corpus before it was included in the list. Just as there is no set size for a corpus (Reppen, 2010), there are no set guidelines for minimum frequency overall. Each list creator can set whatever minimum counts seem appropriate. These minimum counts are arbitrary and certainly impact which words make a list as well as which words do not.

After considering many factors about their corpus, vocabulary list creators have to determine a minimum overall frequency, such as "a word must occur at least 50 times." If the corpus is very large and includes sections for different subjects such as history, biology, and economics, then list creators may also want to set minimum frequency counts for each section, such as "a word must occur at least 10 times in each section of the corpus." Doing so helps ensure that a word that is very frequent in one subject but not in the other areas is excluded from the list, because it is not a general academic word.

Unit of Counting

An important difference between the AWL and many other existing lists is what counts as a word. Lists tend to operationalize the term *word* in one of two ways: a *word family* or a *lemma*. The AWL is based on word families. While both units offer advantages in the creation and then use of a word list, I prefer the use of a lemma, especially for students trying to learn English vocabulary.

You may recall that a **word family** is a headword and all its possible related words using prefixes and suffixes. For instance, the word family for the headword *determine* might include *determine, determines, determined, determining, determiner, determiners, undetermined, predetermined,* and *determination.* Because a word family contains so many members, a word list based on a word family will appear to have a smaller number of items, theoretically making it easier for students. In reality, however, the opposite may be true.

The AWL has 570 word families, which may seem to be a daunting but learnable number of items. However, when the words in these word families are examined more carefully, there are actually 3,112 words in the traditional sense of a word (Hyland & Tse, 2007). Some of these family members have very different meanings (e.g., *react, reactionary, reactor*). Sometimes it is difficult to recognize the connection between word siblings (e.g., *variety, invariably*), especially for speakers of Arabic, Chinese, and other languages that are written in a different script.

Unfortunately for our English learners, a word family with five or more members may have only one member that is truly frequent and therefore only one member worth learning well. Laufer and Cobb (2019) verified this uneven distribution when they found that only a small number of affixes are much more frequent in academic and narrative texts. Their study shows the inefficiency of having students learn multiple members of a word family when many are in fact not common. The bottom line is that making students learn five words in a word family when only one or two appear frequently is bad vocabulary teaching.

Instead of a word family, perhaps a better unit of counting is a lemma. A **lemma** is a word plus its grammatical endings, meaning that it is the same part of speech. The lemma *determine*, which is a verb, includes *determine, determines, determined*, and *determining*. (The noun *determination* and the adjective *determined* are separate lemmas.) A word list using lemmas will naturally have more words in it, so students have more items to learn. However, with lemmas, we can be more confident that each item is worth learning because of its high frequency. In addition, a lemma is easier to learn because it means one thing.

Coxhead (2000) used the word family as the unit of counting. Because the AWL was designed to help students with reading, it was believed students would be able to understand the different family members of a headword if they could see them in their readings. For many learners, especially during reading when students can study a word on a page for a little while, this may be possible. However, research has cast some doubt on this claim.

In one of the more relevant studies, Schmitt and Zimmerman (2002) looked at how well 106 non-native learners of English in three different types of academic programs knew four parts of speech (i.e., noun, verb, adjective, adverb) of 16 words from the AWL. The researchers found that it was rare for learners to know all four forms of a word or none of the forms of a word, so partial knowledge was the norm. They found that learners had more difficulty with adjective and adverb forms.

A 2017 study of 279 Japanese learners at different proficiency levels cast serious doubt on the validity of using the word family to test reading comprehension or create useful word lists. In this study, McLean (2017) examined the receptive understanding of a number of very frequent words and multiple members of their word families. He found solid comprehension of inflectional forms (i.e., the same part of speech: *produce, produces, produced*), but limited comprehension of derivational forms (e.g., *produce, product, productive, unproductive*), even among advanced English learners. In sum, the results of McLean's study provided substantial evidence to support the use of the lemma over the word family. This conclusion was confirmed by Stoeckel and colleagues (2018), who demonstrated that students often had a very difficult time with a word that can function as more than one part of speech.

In his detailed study analyzing word families in vocabulary lists, Brown (2018, p. 51) found that word lists using word families

> ...pose a number of challenges, including the number of word forms with multiple affixes, the number of word forms with more challenging affixes, and the number of word families in which the base word is not the most frequently occurring member. Moreover, the first thousand word families in particular are shown to be challenging.

Besides the assumption that knowing one form in a word family gives students access to all the words or even most of the words in a word family, another limitation in using the word family as the unit of counting is that in many cases, unfortunately, only one or two members of a family may be frequent (Laufer & Cobb, 2019). For instance, the word family for the headword *finance* in the AWL includes *financed, finances, financial, financially, financier, financiers,* and *financing*. The most frequent form is *finance*. It may be easy enough for a student to add *-ed* or *-s* to create a verb, but *financier* is certainly not a frequent word and merits no attention.

By having students learn word families, are we not likely adding to their learning burden for no lexical reason? Some teachers may argue that advanced students need to practice word parts, but what if the form being practiced is not frequent? I find this ironic, since the purpose of a word list is to help students master the vocabulary they actually need, not *might* need or *could* need. A good word list should be of practical, not theoretical, use.

A related problem is when one form is polysemous, sometimes with different parts of speech even. The word *finances* can be a verb or a noun. If an EAP students learns that the verb *finance* (*finances, financed*) means "provide money for," how would that student also know that *finances* can be a noun meaning "funds"? This lexical confusion can be further exacerbated when members of a word family occur in different disciplines or subjects (Hyland & Tse, 2007).

Based on his analysis, Brown (2018) concludes that if students are unable to understand the meanings of individual words within word families, even to a small degree, then lists that consist of word families may provide much lower text coverage than expected, which would also mean less comprehension than normally expected. Schmitt (2000) concurs with these limitations of using the word family as the unit of counting vocabulary.

In sum, using the word family as the unit of counting increases the learning burden for the students, but it does not offer any learning benefits. A word list of lemmas may be more focused and more practical for students. Do not be lured by a list with fewer word families, or turned off by a list with more lemmas. The frequency and usefulness of each item in a list may be much more important than the number of words in the list.

The Real Goal of Any List: Better Coverage

Perhaps the most important test for any potential consumer of a word list is its coverage—that is, the amount of language that the words in a list will actually cover in a student's textbook or a lecture transcript. The AWL provides approximately 10 percent coverage of a text (Coxhead, 2000), which may not seem like such a big number, but Grabe (2009) explains the benefits of the AWL compared to learning general vocabulary, especially for students in their academic subjects. The first 1,000 words from the General Service List (West, 1953)—ignoring the word family vs. lemma distinction—provide an impressive 71 percent coverage of the text on a page. The coverage of the second 1,000 GSL words sadly adds only 5 percent coverage, making the total 76 percent. Each subsequent 1,000 words covers a shrinking percentage, with the next 1,000 adding only 3–4 percent (Nation, 2001). From a pedagogical point of view, at some point, the effort required by the learner or the teacher to master those words is not cost effective in terms of the comprehension benefit. The 570 word families in the AWL provide better coverage than the 1,000 words beyond the 2,000-word level. Therefore, the 2,000 GSL words plus the AWL raises the total coverage to an impressive 86 percent (71 + 5 + 10) (https://www.eapfoundation.com/vocab/academic/nawl/).

How could we show that the AWL provides better coverage of academic material and is not just more difficult words? Researchers have confirmed that the AWL provides a fairly consistent 10 percent coverage of academic works but much smaller coverage of non-academic samples. For example, Coxhead (2000) tested the AWL on a corpus of 3.7 million words of fiction and determined the AWL provided only 1.4 percent coverage. Cobb and Horst (2004) found the AWL provided 11.6 percent coverage of an academic subsection of the Brown corpus (Francis & Kucera, 1982). Hyland and Tse (2007) found that the AWL provided 10.6 percent coverage of a corpus consisting of science, engineering, and social sciences papers. Chen and Ge (2007) found the AWL provided 10.07 percent text coverage of medical research articles. Vongpumivitch and colleagues (2009) found the AWL provided 11.17 percent text coverage of applied linguistics journals. Li and Qian (2010) found that the AWL provided 10.46 percent coverage of finance material.

Other list creators have sought to improve upon this 10 percent figure by using a different corpus, methodology, or unit of counting. Not surprisingly, discipline-specific lists report much higher coverage. The Environmental Academic Word List (Liu & Han, 2015) reported 15.4 percent coverage, while the Medical Academic Vocabulary List (Wang et al., 2008) reported about 20 percent coverage. The highest coverage report that I have seen is by The Chemistry Academic Word List (Valipouri & Nassaji, 2013) with 81 percent coverage; however, this list consists of the highest number of word families at 1400—and remember that a word family can easily have five or more members, so a higher coverage is not so surprising.

While some teachers may be interested in one of the discipline-specific lists, many EAP teachers want a general academic word list, similar to the goals of the AWL. Two such lists that I think merit a great deal of teacher attention here are the New Academic Word List and the Academic Vocabulary List.

The New Academic Word List (NAWL) (Browne et al., 2013a) uses lemmas instead of word families, which is a plus for students. While the AWL assumed knowledge of the GSL, the developers of the NAWL also assumed knowledge of their New General Service List (Browne et al., 2013b; Browne, 2014), which was developed to replace the dated 1953 GSL. In one study comparing the coverage of different lists of a corpus, Palinkašević (2017) found that the NGSL and NAWL give 92 percent coverage, while the older GSL and AWL give only 87 percent coverage for the same corpus.

The impressive Academic Vocabulary List (AVL) (Gardner & Davies, 2014) also uses lemmas instead of word families. Because the AVL is based on a 120-million-word corpus taken from COCA, it is already tagged by part of speech. This grammatical tagging is a powerful tool that allowed the authors to identify lemmas much more easily. For instance, this grammatical tagging clearly distinguishes the lemma *used* as a verb (*she used a car to go there*) from the lemma *used* as an adjective (*she bought a used car*). Gardner and Davies report that the AVL covers almost 14 percent of an academic corpus, compared to the AWL's 10 percent, which is a significant difference indeed. As a newer list, the AVL has not been the subject of as much independent research yet. In one study of university student writing, Durrant (2016) looked at the coverage of the AVL and found half of the words were used very little. However, this discrepancy is most likely because the AVL, like the AWL, is based on texts and reflects vocabulary for reading, but Durrant was looking at the AVL within with student writing, a completely different language modality. If anything, Durrant's study points to the need to consider the vocabulary of academic reading and academic writing separately, not a direct criticism of the AVL.

Research Studies Directly Comparing Academic Lists

Which list is the best? One objective way to compare all these lists would be a research study reporting the coverage of each list for a specific corpus so they may be compared equally. For example, if I am teaching EAP students wanting to improve their English reading skills before they enroll in an undergraduate program, then I should find (or create) a corpus of millions of words from textbooks used in those classes, much as Praninskas did in 1972. Then I would verify the coverage of each list in the corpus by using a vocabulary profiler, such as the one at https://www.lextutor.ca/vp/eng/ (Cobb, T. Web VocabProfile from http://www.lextutor.ca/vp/), an adaptation of Heatley and colleagues' (2002) Range. (See http://www.victoria.ac.nz/lals/staff/paul-nat ion.aspx.)

Unfortunately, very few research studies have been conducted comparing multiple lists. The two lists that appear to have the most published studies comparing them are the AWL and AVL. While the AWL may be the most established EAP word list, the AVL has great potential because it uses lemmas and a much larger and richer corpus.

Newman (2016) compared the coverage of the AWL and AVL in a corpus of 1.9 million words that he created from student textbooks. Thus, this was a good test for both lists, since they were designed from academic texts and were now being tested using practical target texts. Newman's Academic Textbook Corpus (ATC) was created from nine textbooks, representing three subjects (science, history, and math) from three educational settings (middle school, high school, and college or university), so he did a solid job of operationalizing general academic textbook language. The study examined (1) word families from both the AWL and the AVL found in the ATC, (2) words families unique to the AWL in the ATC, (3) word families unique to the AVL in the ATC, and (4) characteristic differences between the AWL and AVL unique word families.

The results suggest that both the AWL and AVL capture high-frequency academic word families that are salient across a variety of academic disciplines and grade levels, but the AVL provides a greater number of unique frequent core academic word families. (Note: Newman had to convert AVL lemmas to word families in order to do a fair comparison between the two lists.) Newman concludes that both the AWL and AVL provide significant coverage of the ATC, but the AVL provides greater coverage on the whole. AVL words appeared more frequently in the corpus. In addition to higher frequency, the range of AVL words in the corpus was substantially higher than that of the AWL.

Following Newman's line of research, Hernandez (2017) also compared the coverage of the AWL and AVL in a corpus mirroring student needs. Instead of targeting textbooks that EAP students would find in content classes, Hernandez examined textbooks used in an intensive English program (IEP), where ESL students typically study English to gain admittance to a college or university. She created an original corpus of 1.6 million words from 50 textbooks being used in the IEP at her university. According to Hernandez, this study used "a practical academic corpus that better represents materials from authentic learning and teaching contexts" (p. 13) than found in many corpus research studies.

In this comparative study, Hernandez counted the occurrences of the AWL and AVL word families in the textbook corpus to determine which list had the best overall coverage, frequency, and range. The results showed a strong presence of both lists in the corpus, but the AVL outperformed the AWL in all three measures.

Commenting on the findings of both these studies, Sandberg (2018) notes that both Newman and Hernandez considered the AVL the better option because it provided better coverage. Sandberg also notes the results might have been slightly biased as the creators of the AVL functioned as their professors and thesis designers.

In a very robust study, Qi (2016) compiled an original corpus of 72 million words from 850 course texts listed in published outlines for undergraduate university courses from 10 different disciplines. In comparing coverage of the AWL and AVL, Qi found an array of differences. For example, certain disciplines had higher coverages by both lists. Corpus material from the Business, Engineering, and Education courses had a higher coverage than materials from Arts and Humanities, Information and Media Studies, and Music. Qi also noted that the longer AVL might be too much of a learning burden compared to the AWL, and suggested that future list makers attempt to limit lists to a more reasonable number of items.

Finally, Hartshorn and Hart (2016) compared the AWL and AVL to identify some of the most important similarities and differences between these two lists. If we look at individual words, both lists have about 3,000 words. However, the AWL omitted all the GSL words, even if they are frequent in academic language, and assumes students will learn all the members of a word family, even if many of those members are not frequent. The AVL does not exclude any of the GSL words just because they appeared in the GSL. If a word is in the AVL, it is because that word occurred frequently in the corpus. Because the AVL uses lemmas, a word will have one main meaning, so though there are more different words in the AVL, the learning word per word is easier. As a teacher, I like the AVL much better because when I explain a word in class, I can explain one meaning for that word and students will learn that meaning. If a word form, such as *present*, has multiple meanings—the verb meaning "give," the noun meaning "a gift," and the adjective meaning "in attendance"—the AVL treats those as three different words (lemmas), and each would be taught in order of frequency in the overall list, not within a word family such as *present*. For both teachers and students, a frequency-based list of lemmas is exactly what ESL specialists should use for English learners.

Additional research is needed to compare the usefulness of these lists. Three of the studies reported here are unpublished master's thesis papers, so as these results are more widely disseminated, perhaps we will see more studies that compare multiple word lists with multiple corpora. For now, many continue to use the AWL as the standard, but the AVL certainly seems to offer students many attractive advantages, including potentially better text coverage and an simpler learning task since each word represents only one part of speech.

7. Using Vocabulary Notebooks

Giving students a list of important academic vocabulary is important, but students need to take responsibility for their academic vocabulary growth. Because learning so much new academic vocabulary is a huge undertaking, students must be involved in this process. As students encounter new academic words in their textbooks, class PowerPoints, or lectures, they should be encouraged to keep some sort of vocabulary notebook of this new academic language. To succeed in improving their English proficiency, they need to become aggressive vocabulary hunters.

Research studies have demonstrated the lexical gains that keeping a vocabulary notebook can produce (Walters & Bozkurt, 2009). However, students are often either unaware of the value of keeping a vocabulary notebook or resist taking on the responsibility for collecting new words (D'Onofrio, 2009; Dennison, 2014), so it is up to teachers to train students to keep a personal record of their new academic vocabulary and explain the benefits.

The main purpose of a vocabulary notebook is to maintain all the new vocabulary in one convenient location. However, writing a word down one time is not sufficient to learn the word; instead, the real value of a vocabulary notebook or any kind of good vocabulary list lies in its potential as a tool for subsequent practice.

Some vocabulary research (Folse, 2006) has shown that the most important feature of vocabulary practice is the number of times a learner mentally touches a word. In effect, the best practice could be the kind that requires students to "touch" the word multiple times, but how is this possible with a student's vocabulary notebook (or a word list)?

A vocabulary notebook can be paper or electronic. Some students prefer a traditional paper notebook, while others prefer apps such as Flashcards Deluxe (http://flashcardsdeluxe.com/Flashcards/), Memrise (https://www.memrise.com/), or Anki (https://apps.ankiweb.net/). These three apps have practice features built into them, but I will show you a way to get multiple practices from a paper notebook if a student prefers a paper notebook.

The first step in keeping a vocabulary notebook that facilitates multiple practice opportunities is choosing what information to write in the notebook. In my experience, most teachers force students to crowd their notebooks with too much useless information about a new word, which is both unnecessary and counterproductive for vocabulary learning.

Batia Laufer, one of the most practical L2 vocabulary researchers (and perhaps my favorite), conducted several experiments (e.g., Laufer & Shmueli, 1997) that showed that when trying to memorize new words, less information is often better. She and others (Chun & Plass, 1996; Knight, 1994; Laufer & Hulstijn, 1998; Prince, 1995) also showed that bilingual notes (translations) are often very good for initial learning of new vocabulary. In L2 vocabulary learning, translations can be very useful (Folse, 2004). In any notebook, I suggest each word have no more than these four pieces of information:

1. the word/item
2. a translation in the student's native language
3. a simple English definition or synonym
4. a common phrase or context using the word, but with a blank instead of the word.

Figure 7.1 shows an entry for the verb *fund* from a paper notebook that was written by a Spanish-speaking student.

Remember that less is okay. Studies have shown learners can remember just as well, if not better, when less information, not more, is presented with new vocabulary.

Unfortunately, some teachers think the opposite. I cringe when I see how much "stuff" some teachers require students to put in their vocabulary notebooks, with some requiring the word, multiple definitions, the part of speech, and complete sentences as examples. With 20–25 words, copying full definitions plus other information is boring and extremely time-consuming, and our students do not have the luxury of extra time. If learners perceive keeping

16. *fund*	*financiar*
give money for	to _____ *a new business*
17. new word	translation
definition or synonym	example with a blank_____

Figure 7.1 Sample Page from a Student Vocabulary Notebook

a vocabulary notebook as just busy work, they will not be engaged in the activity and learning will suffer tremendously.

Furthermore, it is of the utmost importance to remember that the notebook belongs to the student, so teachers should follow a format that a student is likely to actually use for review. To me, a vocabulary notebook is not an assignment; it should be an interactive tool for important learning. The value of vocabulary notebooks is that students can both record and review their new vocabulary. In other words, the recording of the vocabulary is not the end goal. If a student is not going to review the vocabulary in the notebook as well, then there is very little point in keeping a notebook in the first place. For these reasons, I strongly urge teachers to encourage students to keep their vocabulary notebooks simple, which will in turn encourage students to write more words in their notebooks and also facilitate reviewing of the information, potentially leading to greater learning. We should all remember that the real value of a notebook is how many times a learner actually opens it up and reviews new vocabulary.

To encourage multiple reviews, or "touches," a notebook should be neat. The pages should not be cluttered. A sheet of lined notebook paper usually has about 27 lines. If every vocabulary entry uses two lines for the four pieces of information, 13 vocabulary words can appear per page. Since students are more likely to review notebooks that have more white (empty) space, I encourage my students to skip at least one line between word entries. (This is also exactly what I did with my own notebooks when I was studying Spanish, Arabic, Malay, and Japanese.) In fact, skipping *two* lines might be even better. Skipping two lines means only four or five words per page, thus making the page look cleaner while leaving extra space for additional information at some later point.

One example of an additional notation I have made in own vocabulary notebook (or app account) is when I learn a second meaning for a polysemous word. For example, sometimes I later learn an idiom with the vocabulary word, so I will add that. An ESL example could be a student learning the noun *wind* and then later learning the idiom *get a second wind*. The student could write this idiom near the original entry for *wind*. Since many words are polysemous, it could be learning a new meaning for an old vocabulary word. For instance, for the word *just*, most students first learn it means "only," as in *just two people*, but later they learn it also means "recently," as in *I just finished lunch*. If students have additional room in their notebooks from skipping a line, this kind of information could be added quite easily.

Because there are so many words to learn in English, one of our main jobs is to be a coach and keep our students positive and on track. Studying a page of 13 words is a lot. You can review the information for 15+ minutes and never turn the page. Aesthetically, it is a very crowded and uninviting page. Psychologically, this is not very encouraging. However, imagine that this same info is now on three pages because the student skipped two lines between word entries. Learners might feel better if they can accomplish three pages of vocabulary words, as opposed to just one page in the same 15 minutes.

Now that we have discussed what information to include and how to organize it on the pages, let's look at suggestions for rapid review of the material at least four times.

Ask students to create a card (or similar) that is the same width as the notebook page and is big enough to cover up one complete vocabulary entry. Once this has been created, then have students remove half of one of the lines.

Now let's demonstrate how to review using this card. Consider the notebook entry in Figure 7.1 for the verb *fund*.

If you place this card on top of the entry, you will see only the target vocabulary word, so this practices English to native language, which is the easiest of the four options since it does not require you to produce the English word, just recognize it. In other words, it practices recognizing the word *fund*.

The student should start at the top of each page and slide the card down to the next word until all 25 words have been practiced this way first. The owner of this notebook entry would see *fund* and then try to come up with the Spanish translation, that is, a translation into the student's native language.

For the second practice, the student could turn the card horizontally and practice producing the English word from seeing the native language translation. This is the second easiest practice because students must simply supply the word but are not tested on its meaning. Again, the student should start at the top of each page and slide the card down to the next word until all 25 words have been practiced this way first.

The student should start at the bottom of each page so that only the English definition or synonym is exposed. Students are required to produce the English word, but it is from a simple definition or other clue. In Bloom's taxonomy, this is simple knowledge.

Finally, the fourth practice is probably the most difficult in my language learning experience because it requires students to produce the correct English word that will complete an actual example. In Bloom's taxonomy, this is application. This time, the student should start at the bottom of each page and flip the card horizontally so that only the English example is exposed in the bottom right opening.

Of course there are many other tasks that learners could do, but these four are good practice tasks because they require students to interact with the vocabulary in their notebooks multiple times. Multiple encounters are important.

8. Ten Classroom Suggestions for Using Academic Word Lists

Whether students receive a list from their teachers or create their own list in a vocabulary notebook, they need to practice their new academic vocabulary. What can teachers and learners do with a vocabulary list to improve their lexical proficiency?

Teachers use academic word lists in different ways, depending on a variety of factors including their preferred teaching styles, their students, their classroom settings, and objectives. O'Sullivan (2007) wrote a very detailed case study of how one college English program in the United Arab Emirates implemented the AWL to raise their students' vocabulary level. In a study of 193 teachers of academic English, Banister (2016, p. 309) found that

> the AWL is widely used by teachers of academic English, both as a guide for course and materials design and as an instrument recommended for self-study use. English teachers adopt and adapt the list for use with their learners because they believe that it provides a principled basis to focus on general purposes academic vocabulary which is relevant to many learners.

However, the teachers also expressed concerns about the AWL, such as students equating knowing the AWL words with being sufficiently prepared for university work. Some teachers rely too much on the list, while others outright reject the AWL—or any list—because they think lists do not fit in with their communicative teaching methods.

Based on my years of foreign language study as well as teaching English for academic purposes, I offer these ten practical suggestions for effectively using academic word lists with your students.

Suggestion 1: Use a corpus-based word list that matches your students' goals.

There are many kinds of word lists: academic vocabulary, idioms, phrasal verbs, common adjectives, phrases, slang, business terminology, spelling, confusing words, parts of speech (for example, a list of nouns, a list of prepositions), just to name a few. Which kind of list is best for your students?

A good list is one that matches learners' language goals. For example, students who are trying to improve their general conversational skills could use the New General Service List (NGSL) (Brezina & Gablasova, 2015), or perhaps a list of idioms used in conversation. Likewise, students who need to read academic textbooks should use an academic vocabulary list such as the Academic Vocabulary List (Gardner & Davies, 2014), Academic Word List (Coxhead, 2000), or New Academic Word List (Browne et al., 2013a).

Just as with any other learning material, when students perceive the content of a list to be a good fit for their needs, they are more likely to be more motivated in working with the information in that list.

Suggestion 2: Use a corpus-based list.

Lists such as "The 100 Most Frequent Words" or "50 Adjectives You Need to Know" may sound good, but these lists are almost always simple compilations based on one person's intuition and rarely represent actual language usage found in a corpus. By way of comparison, the General Service List (GSL) was painstakingly compiled by Michael West in 1953—pre-internet—from a large written corpus of 2.5 million words (Browne, 2014). Similar to modern professionally compiled word lists, the GSL is the product of a large corpus of actual language. This list was not compiled by one person trying to think of common or useful vocabulary over a few evenings in order to provide content for some random webpage.

Be very skeptical of any list that claims to be the list of the most frequent kind of word, whatever it is, unless this title is backed up with corpus data. In addition, students (and teachers) should consult a corpus-based word list that targets the kind of vocabulary needed for their specific goals in learning English. The words should come from a corpus of the type of language that matches their English needs. If your students want to improve their conversation skills, for example, then the list should come from a corpus that includes real conversations, such as the Santa Barbara Corpus of Spoken American English (https://www.linguistics.ucsb.edu/research/santa-barbara-corpus).

There are in fact many corpus-based lists that have been developed for a variety of language needs. If beginning and intermediate students want to improve their general English proficiency, they could use the General Service List (West, 1953), but they could also use the New General Service List by

Browne and colleagues (2013b) or the New General Service List by Brezina and Gablasova (2015), both of which were designed to replace the older GSL (West, 1953). If students want to improve their academic vocabulary, they could use the AWL (Coxhead, 2000), the Academic Vocabulary List (Gardner & Davies, 2014), or Academic Keyword List (Paquot, 2010).

Suggestion 3: Never attempt to use the whole list at one time.

Like most traditional holiday meals, a word list is simply too big to be consumed in one sitting. Among the more well-known corpus-based lists, for example, the General Service List has more than 2,000 words, the AWL has 3,111 (Hartshorn & Hart, 2016) or 3,112 (Hyland and Tse, 2007) words (or 570 word families), and the Academic Vocabulary List has about 3,000 words. List creators try to limit the size of their lists, but good lists need hundreds of words to provide good coverage, especially if they use lemmas instead of word families. There is no such thing as a truly useful list that has just a few words.

Over the years, I have seen students try to tackle a whole list, starting with A and then B, etc. This is a bad strategy. No one can learn a list of 100 words at one time, let alone 2,000 or 3,000. Therefore, common sense tells us it is just good teaching to break any learning material into manageable chunks. The number of words in this smaller portion can vary according to the learner, the setting, the proficiency level, and many other factors. One suggestion is to aim for a smaller list ranging from 20 to 50 items.

I have seen some teachers balk at 20 as a high number, but I am going to suggest groupings of 20 or maybe even 25 or 30. Our students face such massive lexical gaps in their own knowledge that working with a small number of words like 5 or 10, as I see in many vocabulary lessons, is a mere drop in the bucket. If students should be learning 800–1,000 words and phrases in a course, then grouping these words even in 10s will mean at least 80 lessons, and many courses do not have 80 days to cover 80 lessons. No, students need to do more.

Our English learners' lexical deficit is a huge problem in many ways, including academic performance, social interaction, and employment prospects. A serious student needs to do much more than attend English classes and hope to pick up a few new words here and there. Serious students need to meet the lexical problem head on to overcome this challenge. Attempting vocabulary lessons of 20–25 words daily is one serious response to meet this challenge.

When I work with a list of 25 words, however, I do not expect my students to learn all 25 words perfectly before we move on. Learning a word is a very complicated process, one that is different for different learners and different words (Laufer, 1990; 1994). Sometimes two learners can have very different learning outcomes after meeting the same word in the same lesson. For whatever reason, one student leaves the lesson with only a general notion that *ratio* is connected to numbers or that *conflict* is something negative, while another learner can give an example of a *ratio* or quickly use *conflict* in an original sentence.

Suggestion 4: As much as possible, make learning your smaller list much easier by not including words that look alike or sound alike.

Words that look alike or sound alike can be especially confusing, no matter how different their meanings may be. This is why students who attempt to tackle a vocabulary list alphabetically quickly encounter problems. Imagine trying to learning 10 words that all start with the same letter. If the words look (or sound) similar, it is harder for the learner to remember them because no word is unique.

My graduate students in Japan, for instance, used to confuse *economic* and *economical*. They would often write "The government created a new *economical* plan." (*Economic* is correct here.) They had learned the word family *economic, economics,* and *economical* at more or less the same time. Simultaneously attempting words that look alike or have connected meanings is hard. A better teaching strategy would be to present these words in different lessons. Let one word sink in before the next is introduced.

If you have taught beginning-level English learners, you may have noticed how they often confuse *kitchen* and *chicken*, even though one is a place and the other is an animal. Why does this confusion happen? First of all, the forms of the words are very similar. Both words have two syllables, with primary stress on the first syllable. Both contain the same four phonemes (sounds), but in different order: *kitch(en)* is the reverse of *chick(en)*. Worse, these two words are often encountered at about the same time in the early stages of learning English, so students end up with two very similar vocabulary words that look alike and sound alike vying to enter the lexicon of their new language simultaneously, which is a perfect environment for confusion to occur.

When preparing a smaller vocabulary list for your students, such as 20 AWL words, help minimize word confusion by not including words that look alike (*ratio, rational*) or even words with the same initial letter (*entities, equation, erosion*), the same prefixes (*concentration, conclusion, conference*), or the same suffixes (*adjustment, commitment, equipment*). I would go so far as to avoid words that have a similar visual shape, such as *deny* and *levy*, since both words have four letters, are two-syllable words, begin with a tall letter, end in -*y*, and follow a consonant-*e*-consonant-*y* pattern (Folse, 2004).

The bottom line is that teachers can help learners by choosing the words for these smaller lists judiciously. If you are going to have a list of 20 items, it is important to try to facilitate student learning by not using words that compete with each other for a slot in learners' brains because the words look or sound similar.

Suggestion 5: Do not give students a list of words without first teaching them how to tackle learning the list.

In the end, learning new words is the student's job, not the teacher's, so students need to develop a wide repertoire of vocabulary learning strategies (VLSs) to help with the daunting task of learning a lot of new vocabulary. Even if I as the teacher could teach 24 hours a day, it would still be impossible for me to teach all the words that any group of students—or even one student— needs. For this reason, learners need to assume responsibility for their own learning and train themselves to become what I call "aggressive vocabulary hunters." Remember our students' massive lexical gap. No teacher can possibly teach any learner all (or even most of) the vocabulary that is needed, so the challenge is for students to be able to use a variety of strategies that will facilitate independent learning, including subsequent reviewing, that they can and will do continually.

Sadly, after some teachers locate a vocabulary list they like, they then give a copy to their students with no instructions. Worse, the teacher might say something vague and unhelpful such as, "These are important words. Learn them." Learn them? How? This is not teaching.

In the remaining suggestions in this section, I will give some of my personal favorite ways to use a list as a teacher and as a learner, but for now, the most important message here is that teachers need to introduce learners to some options for tackling any vocabulary list. As you will soon see, there are many different VLSs, yet I am always very surprised when I hear that a student has never heard about a given strategy, such as keeping a vocabulary notebook, or highlighting verbs in one color and adjectives in another.

Students cannot do what they do not know how to do, so the teacher's job here is to acquaint students with a menu of possible VLSs and then help students identify ones that they personally like and can easily implement. Ask students how good each of these strategies is for learning new vocabulary.

1. I focus on the word's definition.
2. I make flash cards with the word, whether paper cards or electronic cards.
3. I connect the new word to a word I already know that has a similar meaning.
4. I translate the word from English to my language.
5. I think of some personal connection between the word and my life.
6. I look up every word in a bilingual dictionary.
7. I use an app like vocabulary.com to help me practice the word.
   (See https://www.inc.com/minda-zetlin/7-mobile-apps-that-will-dramatically-increase-your-vocabulary.html.)

This list of seven strategies is too short to be useful, but it is easy to find extensive lists of VLSs. Perhaps the longest list is in the Strategy Inventory for Language Learning, or SILL (Oxford, 1990). However, just as I would not give students a list of 75 words to learn, I would not give students a list of 75+ strategies, so I would now like to present one successful interactive task that I have used with my own students to introduce VLSs.

No one knows your students better than you do, so after consulting these larger lists, create a list of strategies you think your students might be able to use, based on what you know about your students. For example, older students tend to be less likely to use an app to practice their new words, while younger students may not have the academic skills required to manage their studying or reviewing vocabulary yet. I suggest developing a list of 10–20 potentially appropriate vocabulary learning strategies and then letting your students tell you which ones they already use as well as which ones they would like (and not like) to try.

As a class activity, you can distribute your list to everyone. Allow students time to read the strategies and rate them using this 5-point scale:

4: I use this strategy.
3: I do not use this strategy, but I would like to try it.
2: I am not sure about this strategy.
1: I do not use this strategy, but maybe I will try it if someone can explain why it is good.
0: I do not like this strategy, and I do not want to not try it.

After they have written down their personal ratings, let students discuss their responses. Hearing their peers' comments can be a very good way to introduce students to new strategies they might like to try out. This discussion also makes you aware of how many students do not know about these strategies at all, let alone ever make use of them.

If you are interested in reading more about VLSs, I suggest reading works by Rebecca Oxford (1989, 1990), the original leader of strategy research and creator of the SILL, and an article by Schmitt and Schmitt (1993) dealing with Thai students trying to learn English vocabulary in Thailand.

Suggestion 6: Let students self-assess with your shorter list first.

Although students are in the same class because of similar placement scores, they may actually have shockingly different levels of vocabulary knowledge (Alkhofi, 2015). I try to make use of these differences individually and as a class.

One of my first goals with a word list is simply to raise students' awareness that these new words exist. Before anything, have students rate each word using this four-point scale:

3: I have seen (or heard) this word and know what it means.
2: I have seen (or heard) this word and think I know what it means.
1: I have seen (or heard) this word but do not know what it means.
0: I have not seen (or heard) this word and do not know what it means.

After students have done this individually, I have raised their awareness of each word. When students write a number, they are likely doing so after devoting some thought to the word. This attention requires noticing, which then raises learners' awareness of the word. According to the Noticing Hypothesis (Schmidt, 1990), students are now more likely to pay attention to the word in subsequent encounters because they have already at least noticed it. Thus, this activity not only serves as a pre-test for teachers to see what students know, but also helps students begin the process of learning the words.

After students have determined their level of pre-knowledge of the words, it is time to move to learning something about the meanings of the words. One clever early technique is to let the students teach a few of the words to their peers. Unless you are teaching true beginners or presenting specialized vocabulary that no one has at least seen or heard before, it is very rare to have a class where no one knows anything about one or more words on the list.

Whenever possible, tap into this pre-existing knowledge by letting students teach their peers.

To get students up and moving around, have students stand during the activity. For a word they marked as 0 or 1, they need to find someone who marked the same word as a 2 or 3. Then the student with 2 or 3 should try to explain the word to the student with 0 or 1. In my experience, students end up teaching a few words they already know and also hearing the explanation of a few new words. Students will still have many questions, but that is normal.

At the end of this task, identify three to five of students' least known words. Were students able to find other students who knew or thought they knew the meanings? This activity, which takes perhaps 15–20 minutes for a list of 25 words, is designed to be students' first practice with the words, not their only activity, so do not worry when students still have several unknown words even after completing this task.

As a teacher, I have found this activity to be a very good way to start any lesson that features a vocabulary list. Students have a real reason to speak English as they explain the words they know. Even if they use their L1, they tend to be on task. Furthermore, nothing cements partial knowledge like having to explain that information to another student. As for negatives, I can think of only one potential problem: Sometimes I have had lazy or standoffish students who initially put 3 by every word because they think a high number means I will not call on them to say anything. However, in this activity, putting a higher rating actually means you then have to explain that word to another student. Once students realize this, they tend to self-rate much more accurately.

One additional plus about this activity is that it is a fast way to have students interact with a large number of words (25, for example), but it does not create any papers for you to mark in any way. Students enjoy it because it is a very focused, interactive task with a clear beginning, middle, and end. It features high engagement, high interaction, high speaking, and no grading.

Suggestion 7: When first trying to practice remembering words from the list, assess the difficulty of each word, but do this multiple times over a period of time with increasingly longer intervals in between practices.

After I am somewhat familiar with the new words and their meanings, it is time to practice them to improve my knowledge of the words. One of my first practice activities is simply to go through the list and divide the words into three groups: *words I know, words I sort of know,* and *words I don't know.*

For this task, I prefer to use flashcards. I write each of the words from the list on flashcards. If the list has 25 words, then I will have 25 flashcards for this lesson.

On one side of the flashcard, I write the new word. On the other side, I write a simple definition or a synonym. If I am learning 25 words in a foreign language, I will write the translation into English.

Three examples of simple flashcards are shown in Figure 8.1.

Start with a pile of all the flashcards. In this lesson, I have a list of 25 words, so I have 25 flashcards.

Here are the instructions for students:

All cards are arranged with the word on top so the explanation cannot be seen. Take the first card and say the word out loud: "adjust." Ask yourself: "What does *adjust* mean?" Try to answer the question. Then turn over the card to check your answer. If you answered it right away and got it correct, put it in the I KNOW pile. If you got it correct, but it took you some time to remember it, or if you do not feel so confident about knowing the meaning, put it in the SORT OF KNOW pile. If you missed it, put it in the I DON'T KNOW pile. Continue until you have done this with all 25 cards.

When all 25 cards are now in three piles, pick up the I DON'T KNOW pile and test yourself again. Because you just saw the answers, you may be able to get a few of these correct this second time. If you get one correct, put it in the I SORT OF KNOW pile. Do not put it in the I KNOW pile because your knowledge of this word is not so strong yet. If you miss a word, put it back in the I DON'T KNOW pile.

FRONT		BACK
adjust	*Example from the Academic Word List*	change or move
as well as	*Example from the Academic Keyword List*	in addition to
dinero	*Example from a beginning Spanish class*	money

Figure 8.1 Flashcards for Spaced Rehearsal Practice

Next, pick up the I KNOW pile. Ask yourself these cards again. If you get them right, put them in the I KNOW pile again. If you miss a word, put it in the I SORT OF KNOW or I DON'T KNOW pile, depending on how you evaluate your knowledge of the word.

Finally, do the same process with the words in the I SORT OF KNOW group. If you get a word correct, move it to the I KNOW pile. If you miss a word completely, put in the I DON'T KNOW pile. If you get the word correct but struggle to remember the meaning, keep it in the I SORT OF KNOW pile. Alternatively, this activity can also be done in this order: I DON'T KNOW, I SORT OF KNOW, I KNOW.

This simple categorization task works extremely well for remembering basic meanings of new words.

Suggestion 8: Use spaced repetition to increase your ability to remember new words.

Using flashcards to assess your knowledge of recently learned words and then categorize words as known, partially known, and unknown (Suggestion 7) is a very simple yet effective technique to aid in gaining new vocabulary. However, no matter which practice task we use, people tend to forget new information rather quickly.

In the late 1800s, a German psychologist named Hermann Ebbinghaus conducted several important experiments to quantify our natural forgetting curve. He found that just after learning a lot of information, there is a very steep decline in remembering. In other words, just after trying to learn a lot of information, we usually tend to forget a lot of it, and this process happens very quickly. He also found that whatever he could remember by the second day tended to be information that he could remember for quite a while. However, the problem was how much information we forget so fast.

Ebbinghaus wanted to know if forgetting could be reduced, and through a series of experiments, he calculated how our rate of forgetting could be improved. Through further experiments, Ebbinghaus (1885/1964) found that forgetting could be softened by repeating the new information at particular intervals. This discovery is the basis for a learning technique called **spaced repetition** or **spaced rehearsal**. Bruce and Bahrick (1992) write that this spacing effect was one of the earliest research topics for experimental psychologists such as Ebbinghaus. They go on to note that interest in this effect led to more than 300 investigations in the last century.

Whatever type of practice you do with a set of words, spaced repetition is one of the most powerful techniques for learning large sets of items like new words. Upon reading what spaced repetition is, you may realize that you have made use of this technique many times already without knowing there was a special name for it. In fact, if you have ever crammed for a test of any kind, you most likely use spaced repetition, especially if you did well on that test!

Wikipedia gives a very good general overview of this technique:

> Spaced repetition is an evidence-based learning technique that is usually performed with flashcards. Newly introduced and more difficult flashcards are shown more frequently while older and less difficult flashcards are shown less frequently in order to exploit the psychological spacing effect. The use of spaced repetition has been shown to increase rate of learning.
>
> Although the principle is useful in many contexts, spaced repetition is commonly applied in contexts in which a learner must acquire a large number of items and retain them indefinitely in memory. It is, therefore, well suited for the problem of vocabulary acquisition in the course of second language learning.

Reducing the natural forgetting curve that occurs after learning new information is not just about how many times you practice the information. It is not enough to do the known/partially known/unknown task, for example, five times. To help reduce our natural tendency to forget information, it is important that the recall practices of the information be spaced so that the spacing between the practices gradually increases. What is important is *spaced* repetition, not just repetition.

For example, let's assume you assess your initial memory of the 25 words. Just five minutes later, you repeat the task, regroup the words into three piles, and see which cards are in which pile now.

Using spaced repetition, not just repetition, you would not repeat the task immediately. Instead, go do something else and do it again in an hour. After that, wait one day before your next attempt. Then wait two days. Then wait four days, etc.

What is the best spacing plan? There are many different algorithms based on different models for remembering. What is most important is to increase the spacing between the practice sessions.

There are many software programs and apps for learning new vocabulary, and my one caveat is about spaced repetition. Today's modern technology can easily include spaced repetition, so I would strongly recommend using only programs and apps with spaced repetition built into them as a core feature, not simply an option. Everyone should be benefiting from this scientifically proven memory technique.

Examples of software programs and apps with spaced repetition include Anki, Lingvist, Memrise, and Quizlet. I have worked with Anki and Quizlet. Both have some card sets already prepared, so you can use existing sets or create your own. In my experience, many more teachers have experience with Quizlet, so you may wish to start there because you are more likely to find colleagues who are familiar with it and can coach you through any questions you may have.

All teachers should exploit spaced repetition to help students remember as many new words and meanings as possible. Use only technology that includes spaced repetition as an integral part of its program.

Suggestion 9: Use free practice activities on the internet.

Whichever academic list you are using, you definitely want your students to practice frequently. Ideally, you would like exercises that give students immediate feedback yet do not generate any additional grading or other work for you. There are in fact many good websites offering excellent practice opportunities online.

Here are just a few sites with various practice activities, ranging from flashcards with definitions to practice quiz questions:

AWL: http://www.englishvocabularyexercises.com/AWL/
AWL: https://quizlet.com/subject/vocabulary-academic-awl-exercises/
AWL: https://www.academic-englishuk.com/awl
NAWL/NGSL: http://www.newgeneralservicelist.org/ngsl-for-quizlet-soon
EAWL: https://www.eapfoundation.com/vocab/academic/eawl/highlighter/
ACL: https://pearsonpte.com/organizations/researchers/
    academic-collocation-list/

Suggestion 10: Check the percentage of AWL words in writing.

González (2017) found that lexical diversity is an important factor in successful academic writing. Her results show how knowledge of the AWL words can possibly contribute to student use of mid-frequency vocabulary, an important category for good lexical diversity. Therefore, students should be aware of how much academic vocabulary they are actually using in their own writing.

Many studies (Coxhead, 2000; Chen & Ge, 2007; Hyland & Tse, 2007; Li & Qian, 2010; Dang et al., 2017) show that academic writing usually includes about 10 percent AWL words in it, so students can check their percentage of AWL words in their writing by copying and pasting in into the box at https:// www.lextutor.ca/vp/eng/. This tool will categorize every word in a sample as one of four categories: first 1,000, second 1,000, AWL, or off-list. If the student's writing has about 10 percent AWL words, then it is generally similar to most writing. However, it is important to remember that 10 percent is only a guideline. Durrant (2014; 2016), for example, found considerable variability of academic vocabulary across text types and disciplines.

9. Where Do We Go from Here?

Students learning English in an academic setting need academic vocabulary that will help them function in high school or a university. They need the vocabulary to read a classic novel, write an essay on the disintegration of the Soviet Union, listen to a lecture on the Black Hole, or participate in a class discussion on ethics.

As a teacher, you can now better understand and appreciate your students' problem: they need to learn so much vocabulary but unfortunately do not have a lot of time or English input. You have read about research showing ESL students can speed up their vocabulary growth with explicit instruction and practice, but which vocabulary should they learn?

Corpus-based lists can be very useful here because of their principled selection of vocabulary. Teachers only heard about the AWL in 2000, but in a relatively short period of time, the AWL has become popular. It is now the standard in our field, with many other lists now available. While the AVL and others appear especially promising for EAP students, more empirical research comparing their coverage of real student textbooks and lecture transcripts is needed before we know which are the most useful for our students, opening a promising line of research for future thesis and dissertation studies. In addition, much more specific information, especially corpus-based information, is needed about the three-tiered system used in K–12 programs. Currently, there seems to be no exact list of such words available for educators.

Teachers need to learn about these various lists along with practical ideas for how they should—and should not—be used. As with any teaching or learning tool, there are definitely good ways and bad ways to use a word list. The more vocabulary teaching ideas and techniques educators are exposed to, the better the learning that can take place.

Students need training with good techniques to practice academic vocabulary. To succeed, they need to know that it is their job to assume most of the responsibility for learning English vocabulary. In short, they need to be taught to become aggressive vocabulary hunters.

In general, educators in TESOL need to understand that there may never be a one-size-fits-all academic word list for every student population. We need more research to identify frequent vocabulary in different disciplines.

At the same time, we need to make sure we do not use well-developed lists for the wrong purposes, such as blindly adopting a list like the AWL that was made from a corpus of reading material and then making our students use those words in their academic writing. Without more research, we do not know if the vocabulary in academic reading and the vocabulary in academic writing are the same. Because of the importance of writing in academic success, more research is needed, perhaps along the lines of the research comparing the vocabulary in listening versus speaking or reading (Dang et al., 2017; Liu & Chen, 2019).

Though predominantly a task for students, vocabulary growth also involves researchers and teachers. To advance our knowledge, researchers need to conduct more empirical studies of the effectiveness of the various academic word lists, and teachers need to do action research on the topic of vocabulary teaching and learning in the multitude of language learning settings that exist in language education today. With modern computer knowhow, we now have a way to compile a large corpus of millions of words relatively easily and then use that corpus to systematically identify the most frequent lexical items in that corpus, which can in turn allow us to produce better vocabulary lists to help our students.

BIBLIOGRAPHY

Ackermann, K., & Chen, Y. H. (2013). Developing the Academic Collocation List (ACL) – A corpus-driven and expert-judged approach. *Journal of English for Academic Purposes, 12,* 235–247.

Alkhofi, A. (2015). *Comparing the receptive vocabulary knowledge of intermediate-level students of different native languages in an intensive English program.* Unpublished Master's thesis. University of Central Florida, Orlando.

Anderson, L. W., Krathwohl, D. R., & Bloom, B. S. (2001). *A taxonomy for learning, teaching, and assessing: A revision of Bloom's taxonomy of educational objectives.* New York: Longman.

Atkinson, D. (1993). Teaching in the target language: A problem in the current orthodoxy. *Language Learning Journal, 8*(1), 2–5.

Azar, B. (2007). Grammar-based teaching: A practitioner's perspective. *Teaching English as a Second or Foreign Language, 11*(2), 1–12.

Banister, C. (2016). The Academic Word List: Exploring teacher practices, attitude, and beliefs through a web-based survey and interviews. *The Journal of Teaching English for Specific and Academic Purposes, 4*(2), 309–325.

Baumann, J., & Graves, M. (2010). Commentary: What is academic vocabulary? *Journal of Adolescent & Adult Literacy, 54,* 4–12.

Beck, I., McKeown, M., & Kucan, L. (2013). *Bringing words to life: Robust vocabulary instruction.* New York: Guilford.

Biber, D. (1993) Representativeness in corpus design. *Literary and Linguistic Computing, 8*(4), 243–257.

Biber, D., Conrad, S., & Cortes, V. (2004). *If you look at ...*: Lexical bundles in university teaching and textbooks. *Applied Linguistics, 25,* 371–405.

Bloom, B. S. (1969). *Taxonomy of educational objectives: The classification of educational goals*: Handbook I, Cognitive domain. New York: McKay.

Brezina, V., & Gablasova, D. (2015). Is there a core general vocabulary? Introducing the New General Service List. *Applied Linguistics, 36,* 1–22.

Brown, D. (2018). Examining the word family through word lists. *Vocabulary Learning and Instruction, 7*(1), 51–65.

Browne, C. (2014). A new general service list: The better mousetrap we've been looking for? *Vocabulary Learning and Instruction, 3*(2), 1–10.

Browne, C., & Culligan, B. (2020, January). TOEIC List. Retrieved from http://www.newgeneralservicelist.org/toeic-list/

Browne, C., Culligan, B., & Phillips, J. (2013a). The New Academic Word List. Retrieved from http://www.newgeneralservicelist.org

Browne, C., Culligan, B., & Phillips, J. (2013b). The New General Service List. Retrieved from http://www.newgeneralservicelist.org

Bruce, D., & Bahrick, H.P. (1992). Perceptions of past research. *American Psychologist, 47*, 319–328.

Bushong, R. (2010). The Academic Word List reorganized for Spanish-speaking English language learners. Unpublished Master's thesis. University of Central Florida, Orlando.

Byrd, P., & Coxhead, A. (2010). On the other hand: Lexical bundles in academic writing and in the teaching of EAP. *University of Sydney Papers in TESOL, 5*, 31–64

Chen, Q., & Ge, G. (2007). A corpus-based lexical study on frequency and distribution of Coxhead's AWL word families in medical research articles (RAs). *English for Specific Purposes, 26*, 502–514.

Chun, D., & Plass, J. (1996). Effects of multimedia annotations on vocabulary acquisition. *The Modern Language Journal, 80*(2), 183–199.

Cobb, T. (1999). Breadth and depth of lexical acquisition with hands-on concordancing. *Computer Assisted Language Learning, 12*(4), 345–360.

Cobb, T., & Horst, M. (2004). Is there room for an AWL in French? In P. Bogaards & B. Laufer (Eds.), *Vocabulary in a second language* (pp. 15–38). Amsterdam: John Benjamins Publishing.

Cook, V. (2010). The relationship between first and second language acquisition revisited. In E. Macaro (Ed.), *The continuum companion to second language acquisition* (pp. 137–157). London: Continuum.

Coxhead, A. (1998). The development and evaluation of an academic word list. Unpublished Master's thesis. University of Wellington, New Zealand.

Coxhead, A. (2000). A new academic word list. *TESOL Quarterly, 34*, 213–238.

Coxhead, A. (2011). The Academic Word List 10 years on: Research and teaching implications. *TESOL Quarterly, 45*, 355–362.

Coxhead, A. (2018). *Vocabulary and English for specific purposes research: Quantitative and qualitative perspectives.* New York: Routledge.

Coxhead, A., & Hirsh, D. (2007). A pilot science word list for EAP. *Revue Française de Linguistique Appliqueé, XII*(2), 65–78.

Cummins, J. (2000). Academic language learning, transformative pedagogy, and information technology: Towards a critical balance. *TESOL Quarterly,* *34*(3), 537–548.

Dang, T. (2018). A hard science spoken word list. *ITL—International Journal of Applied Linguistics, 169*(1), 44–71.

Dang, T., Coxhead, A., & Webb, S. (2017). The academic spoken word list. *Language Learning, 67,* 959–997.

Dennison, L. (2014). Lexical notebooks in the EFL classroom. *Issues in EFL, 10*(2), 55–62.

D'Onofrio, G. (2009). The role of vocabulary notebooks in the retention and use of new words. Doctoral dissertation, Concordia University, Montreal, Canada.

Doughty, C. (1991). Second language instruction does make a difference: Evidence from an empirical study of relativization. *Studies in Second Language Acquisition, 13,* 431–469.

Durrant, P. (2014). Discipline and level specificity in university students' written vocabulary. *Applied Linguistics, 35*(3), 328–356.

Durrant, P. (2016). To what extent is the Academic Vocabulary List relevant to university student writing? *English for Specific Purposes, 43,* 49–61.

Ebadi, S., Weisi, H. Monkaresi, H., & Bahramlou, K. (2018). Exploring lexical inference as a vocabulary acquisition strategy through computerized dynamic assessment and static assessment. *Computer Assisted Language Learning, 31,* 790–817.

Ebbinghaus, H. (1964). *About memory: Investigations on experimental psychology.* (H. Ruger & C. Busseniuf, translators). New York: Dover. (Original work published 1885).

Eckerth, J., and Tavakoli, P. (2012). The effects of word exposure frequency and elaboration of word processing on incidental L2 vocabulary acquisition through reading. *Language Teaching Research, 16*(2), 227–252.

Folse, K. (2004). *Vocabulary myths: Applying second language research to classroom teaching.* Ann Arbor: University of Michigan Press.

Folse, K. (2006). The effect of type of written exercise on L2 vocabulary retention. *TESOL Quarterly, 40,* 273–293.

Folse, K. (2010). Is explicit vocabulary focus the reading teacher's job? *Reading in a Foreign Language, 22*(1), 139–160.

Francis, W., & Kucera, H. (1982). *Frequency analysis of English usage.* Boston, MA: Houghton Mifflin Company.

G., R. L. (2013, May 29). Vocabulary size: Lexical facts. *The Economist.* Retrieved from https://www.economist.com/johnson/2013/05/29/lexical-facts

Gardner, D., & Davies, M. (2014). A new academic vocabulary list. *Applied Linguistics, 35*(3), 305–327.

Garnier, M., & Schmitt, N. (2015). The PHaVE List: A pedagogical list of phrasal verbs and their most frequent meaning senses. *Language Teaching Research, 19*(6), 645–666.

González, M. C. (2017). Profiling lexical diversity in college-level writing. *Vocabulary Learning and Instruction, 6*(1), 61–74.

Grabe. W. (2009). *Reading in a second language: Moving from theory to practice.* New York: Cambridge University Press.

Granger, S. (2017). Academic phraseology: A key ingredient in successful L2 academic literacy. *Oslo Studies in Language, 9*(3), pp. 9–27.

Greene, J., & Coxhead, A. (2015). *Academic vocabulary for middle school students: Research-based lists and strategies for key content areas.* Baltimore, MD: Brookes Publishing.

Hartshorn, K., & Hart, J. (2016). Comparing the Academic Word List with the Academic Vocabulary List: Analyses of frequency and performance of English language learners. *The Journal of Language Teaching and Learning, 6,* 70–87.

Havranek, G. (2002). When is corrective feedback most likely to succeed? *International Journal of Educational Research, 27,* 255–270.

Heatley, A., Nation, I.S.P., & Coxhead, A. 2002. *Range and Frequency programs.* Available at http://www.vuw.ac.nz/lals/staff/Paul_Nation

Hernandez, M. (2017). Comparing the AWL and AVL in textbooks from an intensive English program. Unpublished Master's thesis. Brigham Young University, Provo, UT.

Hill, M., and Laufer, B. (2003). Type of task, time-on-task and electronic dictionaries in incidental vocabulary acquisition. *IRAL, 41*(2), 87–106.

Hsu, J.-Y., & Chiu, C.-Y. (2008). Lexical collocations and their relation to speaking proficiency of college EFL learners in Taiwan. *Asian EFL Journal, 10*(1), 181–204.

Hsu, W. (2011). A business word list for prospective EFL business postgraduates. *Asian ESP Journal, 7*(4), 63–99.

Hsu, W. (2013). Bridging the vocabulary gap for EFL medical undergraduates: the establishment of a medical word list. *Language Teaching Research, 17*(4), 454–484.

Hulstijn, J. (1992). Retention of inferred and given word meanings: Experiments in incidental vocabulary learning. In P. Arnaud & H. Bejoint (Eds.), *Vocabulary and applied linguistics* (pp. 113–125). London: Macmillan.

Hulstijn, J., Hollander, M., & Greidanus, T. (1996). Incidental vocabulary learning by advanced foreign language students: The influence of marginal glosses, dictionary use, and reoccurrence of unknown words. *The Modern Language Journal, 80*(3), 327–339.

Hyland, K. (2012). Bundles in academic discourse. *Annual Review of Applied Linguistics, 32*, 150–169.

Hyland, K., & Tse, P. (2007). Is there an "Academic Vocabulary"? *TESOL Quarterly, 41*(2), 235–253.

Katayama, A. (2007). Learners' perceptions toward oral error correction. In K. Bradford-Watts (Ed.), *JALT 2006 Conference Proceedings* (pp. 284–299). Tokyo: Japanese Association of Language Teachers.

Khani, R., & Tazik, K. (2013). Towards the development of an academic word list for applied linguistics research articles. *RELC Journal, 44*(2), 195–214.

Knight, S. (1994). Dictionary use while reading: The effects on comprehension and vocabulary acquisition for students of different verbal abilities. *The Modern Language Journal, 78*(3), 285–299.

Konstantakis, N. (2007). Creating a business word list for teaching business English. *Elia, 7*, 79–102.

Krashen, S., & Terrell, T. (1983). *The natural approach: Language acquisition in the classroom.* London: Prentice Hall.

Kwary, D. A., & Artha, A. F. (2017). The academic article word list for social sciences. *MEXTESOL Journal, 41*(4), 1–11.

Lado, R. (1957). *Linguistics across cultures.* Ann Arbor: University of Michigan Press.

Laufer, B. (1990). Why are some words more difficult than others?—Some intralexical factors that affect the learning of words. *International Review of Applied Linguistics, 28*, 293–307.

Laufer, B. (1994). Appropriation du vocabulaire: Mots faciles, mots difficiles, mots impossibles. *Acquisition et Interaction en Langue Étrangère, 3*, 97–113.

Laufer, B. (1997). The lexical plight in second language reading: Words you don't know, words you think you know, and words you can't guess. In J. Coady & T. Huckin (Eds.), *Second language vocabulary acquisition* (pp. 20–34). Cambridge, UK: Cambridge University Press.

Laufer, B., & Cobb, T. (2019). How much knowledge of derived words is needed for reading? Applied Linguistics. DOI: https://doi.org/10.1093/applin/amz051

Laufer, B., & Hulstijn, J. (1998, March). What leads to better incidental vocabulary learning: Comprehensible input or comprehensible output? Paper presented at the Pacific Second Language Research Form (PacSLRF), Tokyo.

Laufer, B., & Shmueli, K. (1997). Memorizing new words: Does teaching have anything to do with it? *RELC Journal, 28*(1), 89–108.

Lei, L., & Liu, D. (2016). A new medical academic word list: A corpus-based study with enhanced methodology. *Journal of English for Academic Purposes, 22*, 42–53.

Lessard-Clouston, M. (2010). Theology lectures as lexical environments: A case study of technical vocabulary use. *Journal of English for Academic Purposes, 9*, 308–321.

Lessard-Clouston, M. (2012/13). Word lists for vocabulary learning and teaching. *CATESOL Journal, 24*, 287–304.

Li, Y., & Qian, D. (2010). Profiling the Academic Word List (AWL) in a financial corpus. *System, 38*, 402–411.

Lightbown, P. (1985). Great expectations in second language acquisition research and classroom teaching. *Applied Linguistics, 6*, 263–273.

Lightbown, P., & Pienemann, M. (1993). Comments on Stephen D. Krashen's "Teaching issues: Formal grammar instruction." *TESOL Quarterly, 27*, 717–722.

Liu, C., & Chen, H. (2019). Academic spoken vocabulary in TED talks: Implications for academic listening. *English Teaching & Learning*, 1–19. DOI:10.1007/S42321-019-00033-2

Liu, J., & Han, L. (2015). A corpus-based environmental academic word list building and its validity test. *English for Specific Purposes, 39*, 1–11.

Macis, M., & Schmitt, N. (2016). Not just 'small potatoes': Knowledge of the idiomatic meanings of collocations, *Language Teaching Research, 21*(3), 321–340.

Martínez, I., Beck, S., & Panza, C. (2009). Academic vocabulary in agriculture research articles: A corpus-based study. *English for Specific Purposes, 28*, 183–198.

Martinez, R., and Schmitt, N. (2012). A phrasal expression list. *Applied Linguistics, 33*, 299–320.

Marzano, R., & Pickering, D. (2005). *Building academic vocabulary: Teacher's manual.* Alexandria, VA: ASCD.

Mbodj, N., & Crossley, S. (2020). Students' use of lexical bundles. In U. Römer, V. Cortes, & E. Friginal (Eds.), *Advances in corpus-based research on academic writing: Effects of discipline, register, and writer expertise* (pp. 115–134). Amsterdam: John Benjamins Publishing.

McLean, S. (2017). Evidence for the adoption of the flemma as an appropriate word counting unit. *Applied Linguistics, 38*(1), 1–27.

Meisel, J. (2011). *First and second language acquisition: Parallels and differences.* Cambridge, England: Cambridge University Press.

Miller, D., & Biber, D. (2015). Evaluating reliability in quantitative vocabulary studies: The influence of corpus design and composition. *International Journal of Corpus Linguistics, 20*(1), 30–53.

Minshall, D. E. (2013). *A computer science word list.* Unpublished Master's dissertation, University of Swansea, Swansea, Wales.

Nagy, W., & Herman, P. (1987). Breadth and depth of vocabulary knowledge: Implications for acquisition and instruction. In M. McKeown & M. Curtis (Eds.), *The nature of vocabulary acquisition* (pp. 19–36). Hillsdale, NJ: Lawrence Erlbaum.

Nation, P. (1990). *Teaching and learning vocabulary.* New York: Newbury House.

Nation, P. (2001). *Learning vocabulary in another language.* Cambridge, England: Cambridge University Press.

Nation, P. (2006). How large a vocabulary is needed for reading and listening? *Canadian Modern Language Review, 63*(1), 59–82.

Nation, P. (2011). Research into practice: Vocabulary. *Language Teaching, 44,* 529–539.

Nation, P. (2016). *Making and using word lists for language learning and testing.* Amsterdam: John Benjamins Publishing.

Nattinger, J., & DeCarrico, J. (1992). *Lexical phrases and language teaching.* Oxford, England: Oxford University Press.

Nesi, H. (2002). An English Spoken Academic Word List. In A. Braasch & C. Povlsen (Eds.), *Proceedings of the Tenth EURALEX International Congress* (Vol. 1, pp. 351–358). Copenhagen: Center for Sprogteknologi.

Newman, J. (2016). A corpus-based comparison of the Academic Word List and the Academic Vocabulary List. Unpublished Master's thesis. Brigham Young University, Provo, UT.

O'Flynn, J. (2019). An Economics Academic Word List (EAWL): Using online resources to develop a subject-specific word list and associated teaching-learning materials. *Journal of Academic Language & Learning, 13*(1), A28–A87.

O'Sullivan, A. (2007). Integrating vocabulary into an established curriculum. In P. Davidson, C. Coombe, D. Lloyd, & D. Palfreyman (Eds.), *Teaching and Learning Vocabulary in Another Language* (pp. 248–263). Dubai: TESOL Arabia.

Oxford, R. (1989). Use of language learning strategies: A synthesis of studies with implications for strategy training. *System, 17,* 235–247.

Oxford, R. (1990). *Language learning strategies: What every teacher should know*. New York: Newbury House.

Palinkašević, M. (2017). Specialized word lists – Survey of the literature – Research perspective. *Research in Pedagogy, 7*, 221–238.

Paquot, M. (2007). Towards a productively-oriented academic word list. In J. Walinski, K. Kredens, & S. Gozdz-Roszkowski (Eds.), *Corpora and ICT in language studies. PALC 2005* [Lodz Studies in Language 13] (pp. 127–140). Frankfurt, Germany: Peter Lang.

Paquot, M. 2010. *Academic vocabulary in learner writing: From extraction to analysis*. London: Continuum.

Paquot, M. & Granger, S. (2012). Formulaic language in learner corpora. *Annual Review of Applied Linguistics, 32*, 130–149.

Peters, E., & Webb, S. (2018). Incidental vocabulary acquisition through viewing L2 television and factors that affect learning. *Studies in Second Language Acquisition, 40*, 551–577.

Praninskas, J. (1972). *American university word list*. London: Longman.

Prince, P. (1995). Second language vocabulary learning: The role of context versus translations as a function of proficiency. *Modern Language Journal, 80*, 478–493.

Qi, H. (2016). A corpus-based comparison between the Academic Word List and the Academic Vocabulary List. Unpublished Master's thesis. Western University, London, Ontario.

Reppen, R. (2010). Building a corpus: What are the key considerations? In M. McCarthy & A. O'Keefe (Eds.), *The Routledge handbook of corpus linguistics* (pp. 31–37). London: Routledge.

Safari, M. (2018). Do university students need to master the GSL and AWL words? A psychology word list. *Journal of Modern Research in English Language Studies, 5*, 101–122.

Sandberg, A. (2018). Academic vocabulary in Finland-Swedish learners' essays. Unpublished Master's thesis. Åbo Academy, Faculty of Humanities, Psychology, and Theology, Turku, Finland.

Schmidt, R. (1990). The role of consciousness in second language learning. *Applied Linguistics, 11*, 129–158.

Schmitt, D. (2016, March). Defining usefulness: What makes a word list useful? Paper presented at the Annual Meeting of the American Association of Applied Linguists (AAAL), Orlando, FL.

Schmitt, N. (2000) *Vocabulary in language teaching*. Cambridge, England: Cambridge University Press.

Schmitt, N., & Schmitt, D. (1993). Identifying and assessing vocabulary learning strategies. *Thai TESOL Bulletin, 5*(4), 27–33.

Schmitt, N., & Zimmerman, C. (2002). Derivative word forms: What do learners know? *TESOL Quarterly, 36*(2), 145–171.

Simpson-Vlach, R., & Ellis, N. (2010.) An academic formulas list: New methods in phraseology research. *Applied Linguistics, 31,* 487–512.

Sonbul, S., & Schmitt, N. (2010). Direct teaching of vocabulary after reading: Is it worth the effort? *English Language Teaching Journal, 64,* 253–260.

Stoeckel, T., Ishii, T., & Bennett, P. (2018) Is the lemma more appropriate than the flemma as a word counting unit? *Applied Linguistics, 41*(4), 601–606. https://doi.org/10.1093/applin/amy059

Terrell, T. (1977) A natural approach to second language acquisition and learning, *Modern Language Journal, 61,* 325–337.

Valipouri, L., & Nassaji, H. (2013). A corpus-based study of academic vocabulary in chemistry research articles. *Journal of English for Academic Purposes, 12*(4), 248–263.

Vongpumivitch, V., Huang, J., & Chang, Y. (2009). Frequency analysis of the words in the Academic Word List (AWL) and non-AWL content words in applied linguistics research papers. *English for Specific Purposes, 28*(1), 33–41.

Walters, J., & Bozkurt, N. (2009). The effect of keeping vocabulary notebooks on vocabulary acquisition. *Language Teaching Research, 13,* 403–423.

Wang, J., Liang, S., & Ge, G. (2008). Establishment of a medical academic word list. *English for Specific Purposes, 27*(4), 442–458.

Ward, J. (2009). A basic engineering English word list for less proficient foundation engineering undergraduates. *English for Specific Purposes, 28*(3), 170–182.

Watson-Todd, R. (2017). An opaque engineering word list: Which words should a teacher focus on? *English for Specific Purposes, 45,* 31–39.

West, M. (1953). *A general service list of English words.* London: Longman.

Wray, A. (2002). *Formulaic language and the lexicon.* Cambridge, England: Cambridge University Press.

Xue, G., and Nation, P. (1984). A university word list. *Language Learning and Communication, 3*(2), 215–229.

Yang, M. (2014). A nursing academic word list. *English for Specific Purposes, 37,* 27–38.

Youngblood, A., & Folse, K. (2017). Survey of corpus-based vocabulary lists for TESOL classes. *MEXTESOL Journal, 41,* 1–15.

Yoshida, R. (2008). Teachers' choice and learners' preference of corrective feedback types. *Language Awareness, 17*(1), 78–93.

Zhou, A. (2009) What adult ESL learners say about improving grammar and vocabulary in their writing for academic purposes, *Language Awareness, 18*(1), 31–46.

Zimmerman, C. (1997). Do reading and interactive vocabulary instruction make a difference? An empirical study. *TESOL Quarterly, 31,* 121–140.

Printed and bound by CPI Group (UK) Ltd, Croydon, CR0 4YY

13/04/2025